Organizing the Library's Support: Donors, Volunteers, Friends

Edited by D. W. KRUMMEL

University of Illinois
Graduate School of Library Science
Urbana-Champaign, Illinois

Library of Congress Cataloging in Publication Data

Allerton Park Institute, 25th, 1979.
    Organizing the library's support.

    "Papers presented at the Allerton Park Institute
sponsored by University of Illinois, Graduate School of
Library Science, held November 11-14, 1979, Allerton
House, Monticello, Illinois."
    1. Friends of the library — Congresses.   2. Volun-
teer workers in libraries — Congresses.   I. Krummel,
Donald William, 1929-   II. Illinois. University
at Urbana-Champaign. Graduate School of Library Sci-
ence.   III. Title.
Z681.5.A44   1979   021.7   80-14772
ISBN 0-87845-054-8

ALLERTON PARK INSTITUTE

Number 25

Papers presented at the Allerton Park Institute

Sponsored by

University of Illinois
Graduate School of Library Science

held

November 11-14, 1979
Allerton House
Monticello, Illinois

CONTENTS

The Allerton Park Institute on Library Friends

On November 11-14, 1979, the University of Illinois Graduate School of Library Science sponsored the twenty-fifth annual Allerton Park Institute at Robert Allerton Park near Monticello, Illinois. This silver jubilee conference was devoted to the work of auxiliary groups which support libraries through donations of time, enthusiasm, political encouragement, money, and books.*

The importance of the topic was evidenced by a capacity registration for the institute. No less gratifying was the wide geographic spread of the ninety-one participants; in all, thirty-two states were represented, with 70 percent of the registrants coming from more than 500 miles away. (Allerton Park Institutes are used to having Illinois as the home state of the largest number of registrants, but it was a pleasant surprise this year that Delaware came in second, Georgia third, and Oklahoma fourth.) The number of small libraries represented, both academic and public, is all the more impressive, and evidences the depth of interest in the topic today.

The reason for the interest is not obscure. Friends groups are springing up across the country in recognition of the classic adage about "friends in need." In the auspicious times of twenty or even ten years ago, libraries could go merrily on their way fulfilling their missions. As Euripedes could say of his Orestes, "When fortune smiles, who needs friends?" Happily, it seems likely to be our fate to avoid the disasters of the House of Agamemnon; but oh, how times have changed! In our days of rampant inflation, tax revolts, pressures for more outreach, more computers, better collections, and better services, we prefer to recall another ancient adage about needing all the friends we can get. We are therefore fortunate that we were building up great amounts of residual good will during those happy days of sputniks and Camelots. The value of ancient and long-standing friends is amply documented by adages which scarcely need to be repeated here (readers presumably do not wish to be told once again about King James's old shoes or

---

* This text is an expansion of the summary remarks at the conference, which were mercifully shortened by the need for participants to catch departing transportation. At that time, I promised to include an anthology of quotations relating to friends which had not, to my knowledge, been expressed during the course of the institute. These can be verified in several standard books of quotations.

1

Benjamin Franklin's old dog). More to the point: in our days of need, what should we be doing to call on our friends indeed?

The problem begins at home: one makes friends by being a friend. For librarians the notion is at once perfectly natural and disturbingly revolutionary. Notwithstanding the occasional Scrooge or Scroogess whom one might still encounter on a bad day, the librarian's philosophy of today is clearly one of service. But the same philosophy has also held that God in his heaven (or the next best thing, a few godly magnanimous patrons, or the local or, more recently, the federal government) would take care of us. The thought that librarians should pass the hat among readers, associates, fellow librarians, colleagues, and well-wishers — nonsense! Perhaps what we must learn is that there is nothing dishonorable, nothing demeaning, nothing perverse or perverting in the acceptance of charity. It can all be done as quietly as a waiter collecting a tip, as unassumingly (i.e., as assumingly) as an usher taking the offering in church, as stylishly (and with as much formal stylization) as a concert singer accepting a bouquet. The notion that the acceptance of charity is debasing is hard to dispel — for those who do not know the reciprocal dignity of charity. The librarian must learn to ignore the innuendos of the occasional mischievous donor, as well as to question ill-conceived promotional literature which plays down the dignity of the donor. In fact, as the library profession at large seems to be coming to realize, the most forward-thinking of our institutions have been passing the hat for many years — usually with no noticeable evidence of concomitant corruption, and often with magnificent collections, buildings, programs, and good will to show for their efforts.

The problem does begin at home, within the library. Librarians who have been prime movers for friends groups within their institutions will know the diverse sentiments which have been their major obstacles. Does it really make any sense to implement time-motion studies in order to release a staff member to pour tea at a reception? Can the grumbling reader possibly be appeased by an appeal for funds, when he is already asking ten times more than the library ought to be providing? Those librarians who have heard such sentiments will understand how the proposal of the present topic for an Allerton Park Institute was greeted by a nearly equal mixture of strong support and antipathy. The librarian already has too much to think about in running things as they ought to be run; why take on one more time-consuming responsibility?

"Amici fures temporis," Francis Bacon warns us: "friends are the thieves of time." They also want things in return as well — perhaps not the formal determination of policy ("pay the piper, call the tune"), but at least a word of gratitude (sometimes profuse words), a few perquisites, supervision of their volunteer activities, and above all, a sympathetic ear (usually involving a hidden agenda which, for better *and* worse, does indeed concern library policy). It takes strong librarians, and it does, in variable and immeasurable ways, divert the resources of the library as a functioning institution. The basis for the librarian's effort has to be a profound belief that the effort is worth the while. One observation made a particularly strong impression on the participants when it was expressed at Allerton House — to half of them because it was to be taken for granted and did not need stating, and to half of them because it was an unthinkable heresy: library staff members should be encouraged to join their own friends groups.

Some of the reservations about an Allerton Park Institute on library friends do touch on a basic matter: fears were expressed that there would not be enough content to fill an institute. These seem to have been allayed for those who attended the conference (several registrants, in fact, felt that the program allowed too little time for absorption and interaction). More to the point was the question of whether the special needs of librarians were really appropriate for the attention of an academic teaching and research university: aren't they all practice and no theory, so as to call for a "workshop" rather than a formal "institute"? Is there any methodology, any paradigm involved in library friends work?

Is there any theory behind library friends work, or is it all practice? As organizer of and prime mover behind the institute, I had hopes of turning up some principles. They may indeed exist; but if the papers presented here are any indication, they are a good way off. We do now have Edward Holley's five conditions and four myths, Sandy Dolnick's ten commandments, Tem Horwitz's fourteen points, and Marianne Briscoe's four categories of members. These can, of course, generate some very nice multiple-choice questions for machine-graded exams, but the few universals which seemed to be emerging all receded under cross-examination. It was agreed that the head librarian needed to be involved — until several participants described instances where activities were flourishing in spite of administrative apathy. On the other hand, it was generally agreed that administrative antipathy would be disastrous. What formulas are appropriate for a dues structure? The question was asked a number of times at the institute, and ducked just as many times, leaving us back where we were in 1659, when James Howell observed, "Make not thy friend too cheap to thee, nor thyself too dear to him." How much of the income should be spent on membership perquisites, or on the development of a larger membership?

A few universals did emerge, most notably the need for personal relationships. Friends require, if not always individual cultivation, at least some feeling that they are individually worthwhile to the cause of the library. Beyond this (as the old Harvard gentleman's rule goes), "there aren't any rules until you've broken them." May it not be a case of our not having yet developed enough expertise to formulate the rules? There will surely be more practices in time, good at least for tomorrow if not forever; and library friends organizers will be well advised to become part of the informal community of concerned colleagues. One more "invisible college" will not likely be able to find definitive answers, but it will be essential as a grapevine for advice, and a sounding board for proposals on policy development; such being the case, the Friends of Libraries U.S.A. is as auspicious as it is important. But as for the rules of the game, it seems best here to quote William Penn: "There can be no friendship where there is no freedom. Friendship loves a free air, and will not be fenced in straight and narrow enclosures."

This is not to say that the development of friends groups is not here to stay, or that it is not beneficial. Indeed, those of us who train librarians will be well advised to recognize the importance of this work; but where in our already crowded curricula? A full course on the subject would seem at once both too wasteful and too impractical. The work is far removed from the conventional coverage of either "user studies," or budgeting, or public services, or administration. Scattered admonitions throughout the curriculum would be as useful as a drill sergeant warning new recruits that they will some day be shot at. At the same time, the subject does need to be seen as a pervasive one. The thought of defining, and then recruiting for our library schools, what one might call "friendly types" is simply appalling. I left the institute fully convinced that the topic is vitally important, but as a teacher of future librarians I can see my presentation of the topic being of the decidedly unhelpful form which says, in effect: "you'll need to do it; it's more enjoyable than you might imagine; there is no way to anticipate your problems; so get in there and have fun."

The institute did tend to confirm what might be called the basic unity of the library friends community. In planning the program, the Monday afternoon and evening sessions (Mathews, Wedel, and Seaton) were directed essentially toward public and school libraries, where the basic objective is program support (notwithstanding the strong collection-oriented friends groups in large cities like Detroit, Philadelphia, and Cincinnati). In contrast, the Tuesday afternoon and evening sessions (Briscoe, Holman, and Mosher) were directed essentially toward academic and nonprofit special libraries, where the main objective is collection development (notwithstanding the need of all of these libraries for program support as well). As delivered, however, these papers instead seem rather to address a common goal of all libraries. Equally surprising — and basically a pleasant thing to behold, despite a few awkward moments during the institute — was the indistinguishability of the librarians from the many nonlibrarians who attended the institute, either as active friends of libraries or, in several instances, even as trustees. Friends groups, like most other programs today, depend for their success on prime movers, whether they come from the small world of the library staff or the large world of the library's public.

Tryon Edwards has made a useful distinction between remedial and preventive charity: "The former is often injurious in its tendency; the latter is always praiseworthy and beneficial." The positive approach — whether it emphasizes the classic "margin of excellence" concept, or the recent concern for useful activities no longer within the reach of regular budgetary allotments — is obviously the healthy one. For this reason, it seems to me utterly wrong that a session should have been devoted to the future of library friends; and the absence (to my knowledge) of any references to light at the end of the tunnel is evidence mostly that our faith is in the right place. The faith which builds libraries is simply not the faith which extrapolates fixed laws of human behavior. Rather, it is the quite genuine, even naïve, belief that a change of officers every few years has to be a good thing, not because the new officers will necessarily be poorer or richer, younger or older, less or more educated, but mostly because redefinition is part of the process of staying alive.

Through these essays, however, runs a commitment to a classic conception of the library. Books are the crucial artifact, but not the only one. There does, however, seem to be a common acceptance of the role of the library as a center for all kinds of civilizing activities, involving theater and concerts, films and recordings, grand pianos, even gourmet dinners. The incredulous apathy of the professional library staff member is understandable; after all, his library school training taught him Ralph Ellsworth's Rule 17 for library buildings: "Challenge all proposals to house a museum, art gallery, public auditorium, or any other non-library community activity in the library building."[1] The faith which makes great library friends groups is still a faith in the values which the library has most meaningfully conveyed — intellectual and artistic content, one would like to think, quite apart from the medium involved, be it a document on paper, film, or computer, visually or auditorily perceived.

Victor Hugo, witnessing the destruction of one Paris library in the Communard siege of 1871, was compelled to produce a splendid poem on the cause of books and libraries. There is more than a touch of sympathy in the apology he puts in the mouth of the arsonist: "I can not read." More to the point is Hugo's own ringing assertion:

> A library implies an act of faith,
> Which generations still in darkness hid
> Sign in their night in witness of the dawn.[2]

If the library itself is our civilization's collective signatory act, the signature on our library friends membership cards expresses the individual faith of those who make up that society today.

The reader of these papers, meanwhile, on several occasions will be usefully reminded of the precise dates of the institute. The sessions took place between noon on Sunday, November 11, and noon on Wednesday, November 14, 1979; Thursday morning began the much-heralded White House Conference on Library and Information Services. A number of persons who attended the institute, including at least two of the speakers, were also planning to attend the conference. As of the time of editing of these papers, there is no way to know what to expect from the conference. No doubt a few of the remarks in these papers would have been stated in a slightly different way from the retrospect of even three or four months; one hopes that the erring will have been on the side of understatement. In several of these papers in particular, the reader will sense the spirit of anticipation, largely one of guarded optimism; the exact time of the institute, in any event, is an important fact for the reader to remember.

In the preparation of these papers for publication, the sequence of delivery has been reordered so as to bring together at the beginning those papers concerned with library friends in general, then those devoted to specialties which concern all kinds of nonprofit organizations involved in public support. One paper delivered at the institute is not included here, being more in the nature of informal background comments with extensive discussion afterward. Gratitude must be expressed to Robert L. Reid of the University of Illinois Foundation for his helpful discussion of legal matters, including bequests, tax appraisals, and, above all, deferred giving programs. The texts of other papers as presented here consist mostly of the prepared talks; it was unfortunately not possible to collect or to summarize the scheduled discussions which followed them, much less the unscheduled discussions which took place at the receptions, around the table of friends publications on exhibit, and on the formal and rustic paths of Robert Allerton Park.

Special thanks are due to the University of Illinois Library Friends for sponsorship of the opening reception of the institute, and to the members of the institute planning committee, which included Prof. Walter C. Allen of the Graduate School of Library Science, Dr. Scott Bennett of the University Library faculty, and Mrs. W. Peter Hood and Mrs. Earl W. Porter of the University of Illinois Library Friends.

D. W. KRUMMEL

NOTES

1. Ellsworth, Ralph. "Library Buildings." *In* Ralph R. Shaw, ed. *The State of the Library Art.* New Brunswick, N.J., Rutgers University, Graduate School of Library Service, 1960, vol. 3, pt. 1, p. 28.

2. Hugo, Victor. "Juin," from *L'Année terrible* (1871). Quoted *in* Alexander Ireland. *The Book-Lover's Enchiridion.* 3d ed. London, Simpkin, Marshall, 1883, p. 297.

EDWARD G. HOLLEY

The Library and Its Friends

As cultural and educational institutions, libraries have, from the very beginning of their existence in this country, enjoyed the encouragement and support of a host of friends. This has been true no less for public institutions than for private institutions. It is clear from any reading of the historical record that important libraries do not come into being without the vision, imagination, and determination of individuals who not only give support themselves, but also encourage others to do so. This tradition of contributing books, and funds for books, has an especially long history in higher education as demonstrated most clearly in two of the country's oldest universities — Yale and Harvard.

The late James T. Babb, for many years Yale's librarian, told with relish the story of the founding of Yale College. According to tradition, ten Congregational ministers met in the home of the Reverend Samuel Russel in Branford, Connecticut, in 1701. Each clergyman brought with him some of the choicest volumes from his personal library. As the ministers gathered around a table in Mr. Russel's home, each one placed his particular contribution thereon and intoned these solemn words: "I give these books for the founding of a college in this colony."[1]

As is true about legends surrounding the founding of most colleges, this one is probably apocryphal. Yet Mr. Babb used it to point up an important fact for his donors: the tradition of contributing books and book funds to Yale is an ancient and honorable one. Babb could be especially sanguine about that tradition. During his tenure as Yale Librarian, the Beinecke family gave Yale around $11 million to build a magnificent rare book library, and have subsequently provided additional millions to endow it. Other "sons of Eli" have been equally generous to Yale, as any annual report of the librarian well demonstrates. Babb's successor, Rutherford D. Rogers, does not hesitate to list in detail the annual contributions to book and other funds. One can only look with envy at the latest *Report* (1977-78) where, for example, four donors gave $73,734 for the endowment of the Librarian's Discretionary Fund.[2] Even with today's inflation, the income from that amount gives a librarian flexibility he would not otherwise have. Other gifts for endowment and expendable funds fill six pages of the li-

9

brarian's *Report,* the amounts ranging from $5 to $494,279. Friends and alumni are thus keeping up the ministers' splendid example. Presumably, the tradition of library gifts so carefully nurtured at Yale stems from a recognition that the library plays a central role in Yale's past and present eminence.

Old and famous as Yale tradition is, however, it is not the oldest in the country. That distinction belongs to Harvard, whose name was changed in grateful recognition of John Harvard's bequest of 400 books and half his estate in 1638. Although the Harvard Library burned down in 1764, with a loss of about 5000 volumes, as early as 1773 the library had regained its original number of books and by 1800 had become the nation's largest university library, a position it has continued to maintain. The Harvard libraries, with collections today totaling about 10 million volumes, have benefited greatly from the gifts of donors too numerous to mention. Any record of contributions to libraries cannot ignore the substantial gifts for book funds, for endowment, and for buildings which friends of Harvard have provided so generously in the years since World War II.

In these opening remarks, then, I want to suggest that it is no accident of geography or piety that Harvard and Yale today have the largest university libraries, though both geography and piety may have helped. From the beginning there has been a recognition of the principle that books and libraries are indispensable for the advancement of scholarship, culture, and learning. And I add, lest the point be lost subsequently in the discussion, that no library has ever achieved significance without the support of those who understand that principle, whether they be librarians, faculty, donors, administrators, or legislators. From the Library of Congress to the libraries of Illinois, Michigan, or North Carolina, to Davidson College or the New York Public, or even the small Chapel Hill Public Library, the same principle applies: libraries exist because of those who understand their mission, who are sympathetic to that mission, and who give it their moral, political, and economic support.

Splendid you may say, but my library is not Yale or Harvard. Nor do I have long tradition, wealthy alumni, or development directors to assist me. Is it possible for *me* to rally friends of libraries to my aid and to increase the understanding of the role my library plays in the school, the community, the college, or university? That is the important question and one which should receive answers from the speakers who will follow me. If I understand the world of federal, foundation, and individual grants, I suspect that the answer will be: "Yes, there is a great deal of talent, time, and money in this incredibly affluent country which can be devoted to the library cause; but the cultivation of such resources requires careful planning, selecting achievable goals, and the commitment of much time and effort on the part of the library staff."

Before speaking in broad terms about that support, I will relate an incident which occurred when I first became director of the University of Houston Libraries in the early sixties. In the interviews prior to my selection, everyone had assured me that the potential for library development was beyond my imagination — and that prediction was ultimately realized. When I accepted the directorship, I was keenly aware of the need for an instant research library; however, with only a newly-minted Illinois Ph.D. in my hands, acquiring one seemed "the impossible dream." Nevertheless, I approached the money-raising vice president that fall with the brash suggestion that we needed to raise $10,000 immediately. Although he didn't exactly say "So what else is new?" I did understand the message which came out of that meeting. He gave me a list of prominent Houstonians who could help me, cited their backgrounds and involvement with the university, and suggested a renewal of the Friends of the Library organization. That I left disappointed certainly is an understatement. No vision ever had such an appearance of unreality as did that dream of instant wealth to be garnered for the good and noble cause of the University Library. But it was a valuable first lesson, perhaps all the more so for coming so early in my career. Even Texans do not part with their money casually, and a librarian must expect to build his or her support group over time.

What I subsequently learned in my ten years in Houston was that there were many persons of wealth, or persons connected with persons of wealth, who were ready and willing to provide for civic needs, which included specifically the need for a research library at the University of Houston. I also discovered that, although development directors and university administrators might introduce me to some of these persons, the basic task of explaining what the library wanted and how potential donors could help achieve library goals would be mine, with the assistance of the library staff. Any librarian who believes he or she can depend upon other persons for the primary task of interpreting the library to those who have the resources to help is living in a world of unreality, from which the awakening can sometimes be painful indeed.

I will cite just one example. The vice president for development had learned, through one of his lawyer friends, that a mother and daughter wished to honor the memory of the father, a founder of one of the major insurance firms in Houston. I was asked to write up not more than three pages setting forth our most significant need and how this might be used to memorialize the gentleman in question. Naturally this request occurred at an inconvenient time, when I was in the midst of other projects. Nonetheless, after consulting the staff, I decided that the foundation stone of a research library is its national and trade bibliography collection. We decided to ask for approximately $50,000 (the suggestion was from $25,000 to

$50,000 — one never asks for the lower figure) to establish a named bibliography collection. In as few words as I thought could convey why a good bibliographic collection is important, I sent my proposal and then waited. And waited. And waited. At about the time I had completely given up hope, a year later as I recall, I received word that the vice president and I were to accompany his lawyer friend to tea at the apartment of Mrs. Joseph W. Evans to talk about the proposal. Mrs. Evans and her daughter, Mrs. Fletcher Pratt, had a few questions about the project. They wanted to be sure chiefly that the bibliography collection really would be useful, and asked how I proposed to use the money they would provide. It was a genuine pleasure to inform them of the value of national and trade bibliographies for research and scholarship, to suggest who could be expected to use the collection, and to point out the continuing importance of this investment in the University of Houston Library. Mrs. Evans's response was immediate: "Alice, don't you think we should go ahead and write a check now for part of the money so that Dr. Holley can get started?" The check was written; I was shortly on the phone to my friend, Harold Mason, at Kraus Periodicals; and we were soon filling the shelves with volumes from a bibliographical collection Harold had recently purchased from a society in Great Britain. Mrs. Evans's gift provided the impetus for strong support from many other interested citizens during my decade as director of the University of Houston Libraries.

This story illustrates several points I want to make:

1. the library's importance as seen by the university administration,
2. the value of contacts by the development office,
3. the advantage of developing a list of projects in priority order for the time when resources may become available,
4. the need to match the donor's interests and the library's needs, and
5. the crucial discussions in which the interaction between the librarian and the donor take place.

Mrs. Evans and I became good friends after that, and, although she never gave large sums of money again, her support and encouragement meant much to me. This points up another lesson: working with the library's friends can often be personally rewarding. Emily Scott Evans was a gracious and charming woman whose father had been president of the Mercantile Society Library in St. Louis. She took an interest in the library, talked about it to her friends, and always had a personal interest in the Holley family. Sometime after she had given us the funds for the Joseph W. Evans Bibliography Collection, Mrs. Evans and Mrs. Pratt visited the campus at my invitation to see what we were doing with their money. She was fascinated by the place and especially enjoyed watching the students. As we were leaving the office of President Hoffman, Mrs. Evans turned to him and said, "When I gave the money for the collection in my husband's memory, I thought I would just write out the check and that would be that. I never realized how much genuine pleasure I would derive from the collection and from being associated with the University of Houston."

All of us who have rattled the tin cup, whether quietly or aggressively, can relate similar experiences. Individual donors respond to a challenge to be part of an important cultural or educational institution, and also to the personal touch. David Kaser pointed out in an article "The Golden Touch; or the Gentle Art of Raising Money" that the cardinal rules in seeking outside funds are consistent with simple courtesy and common sense.[3] One must know the donor, have a specific project in mind, explain the opportunity to participate in an important project of value to society, and then keep the donor informed about the outcome of the project. As one development officer told me when I inquired about thanking the donor of a somewhat sensitive gift, "you can never thank a person too much."

I know that there are experiences with donors that do not turn out well, and many of us have the scars to prove it. Mrs. Evans was an exceptionally charming woman, but I must confess that most of the donors with whom I've been associated have also been easy persons to deal with, though they didn't always do what I wanted them to do. For example, our donor of Bibles, the late Henry Rockwell, either responded immediately with a check or totally ignored my "opportunity" letter. Peggy Schiffick responded, after I had recited my litany of needs, "Ed, they all sound like wonderful projects, but what I'm really interested in is the environment. Do you suppose there's something in that area that we could do for the library?" Of course there was, and the contributions of the Schifficks to the University of Houston over the past decade have been especially important in this newly emerging field.

Only three persons proved really difficult during my decade at Houston. One was a lady who wished to memorialize her husband with a special room and a small collection of books for $20,000. We were never able to convince her that what she wanted was neither in the library's nor in her own best interests. The library's policy, of course, was not to set up small special rooms with isolated collections which were difficult for students to locate. There was also a gentleman who shepherded the millions in his uncle's foundation. He was tiresome, needed more ego-massaging than I had time for, gave us insignificant items from time to time, all of which called for the kind of gratitude I felt beyond my capability. However, I understand those long years of patience and trials with the gentleman have eventually paid off for my successors. I wish them well, and feel partially compensated for those long, dull conversations over the telephone. The third person had a very fine collection but was trying to escape both the worst consequences of the Internal Revenue Service and the greediness of his ex-wife. The university paid for his generosity many times over through the unreasonable demands he made on the staff.

Up to this point I have stressed the importance of individual donors to libraries. However, I wonder if the reader is fully aware of the contributions made by foundations and other major donors to libraries in the past decade. As Ann Prentice has pointed out in her essay in the recent *Funding Alternatives for Libraries,* the period of the 1960s and early 1970s was one of impressive federal grants.[4] This was also a period of significant foundation grants. Because relatively little has been written about foundation gifts to libraries, I had my research assistant go through editions of *The ALA Yearbook, The Bowker Annual,* and *Library Literature* of the past decade and compile data on gifts of more than $225,000 to libraries. Included were three government agencies — the National Endowment for the Humanities (NEH), the National Science Foundation, and the National Institutes of Health — plus regrants from the Council on Library Resources (CLR), which itself received $11 million from the Ford Foundation. As we all know, the library reporting systems are poor, and these figures do not represent all the large grants made to libraries. However, those gifts that were reported do have some relevance to this discussion. The reported totals of gifts ranged from $3.4 million in 1976 to $34.4 million in 1974. Since the latter year was the year in which the Rockefellers gave $4.5 million to Rockefeller University for the Rockefeller Archives, and Ford gave $6 million to CLR, the figures are skewed for that year.

Who were the major contributors of these large grants? The largest was the Andrew W. Mellon Foundation with almost $17 million, followed by Ford's $14.1 million (of which $11 million was for CLR), and Kresge's $11.3 million (see table 1). Some of the large foundations appearing in the table make grants for very specific purposes. Kresge, Dana, and Seeley G. Mudd provided funds for buildings, the Vincent Astor Foundation gave $7 million of its $7.5 million as a challenge grant to the New York Public Library, and the Bush Foundation gave money mostly to Minnesota colleges.

Where did the grants go? Table 2 gives the answer, with construction accounting for almost $60 million, followed by about $29 million for automation. One of the strong supporters of libraries was the Andrew W. Mellon Foundation, under the leadership of former Harvard president Nathan Pusey. The Mellon grants were not narrowly confined, but covered many worthwhile activities: buildings, library development, bibliographic access to collections, internships for minority librarians, and library networks.

Who received more than one grant? Table 3 shows that except for Davidson College, which was raising money for a new building, the list of

TABLE 1. MAJOR GRANTS TO LIBRARIES, IN THOUSANDS OF DOLLARS*

Agency	1969	1970	1971	1972	1973	1974	1975	1976	1977	1978	1979
Vincent Astor Foundation								1000	500	5000	
Bush Foundation	250	600	1200		225	540				1400 (2)	
Carnegie Corporation of New York	233			846 (2)	909		300			600	500
Council on Library Resources		250	400		698						
Charles A. Dana Foundation, Inc.	300		600		320						600 (2)
Ford Foundation	350	816 (2)	5997 (4)			6467 (3)				500	
Kresge Foundation		500		2000 (3)	1500 (3)	3730 (6)			3600 (5)		
Andrew W. Mellon Foundation		1500 (2)	3550 (9)	4800 (9)	750	3700 (6)			1570 (4)		1000
Seeley G. Mudd Fund			2750		4425 (4)	2300 (2)				400	
Rockefeller Foundation	350					5163 (2)			1500	1364 (2)	
Alfred P. Sloan Foundation									300	325	500

* Numbers in parentheses indicate number of grants made that year.
Note: Sums are for funds listed on master sheets; therefore, a total picture of all grants awarded to libraries during 1969-79 is not provided. Only gifts of more than $225,000 are included.

TABLE 2. Purposes and Amounts of Grants (In Thousands of Dollars)

Purpose	1969	1970	1971	1972	1973	1974	1975	1976	1977	1978	1979
Automation	350		1082	768	948	8280	682	2389	3677	1579	2600
Collection development	2950	1266	2758	520		250	300		560	3500	394
Construction	4698	8736	9568	5364	8059	12,440	3800		4800	1650	300
Cooperation	233			450	450						
Endowment	500		527	1500		1500				5650	
Extension of services			247	1082	400		625		522	300	
General support	1475	1205	5696	1880	2086	6942		1000	8100	515	
Library education				233							320
Miscellaneous						700	894			1249	
Preservation of rare books	1249	1249	1007	400	459	2040			2350	1052	

those receiving several grants is quite predictable. One might be inclined to say, in the words of that old doggerel, that the rich get richer, and the poor get poorer and the music goes round and round. That is far from the truth, of course, as anyone familiar with the gentle art of money raising can testify. Not shown in any of these figures are the large sums of money the National Women's Committee of Brandeis University raises each year for the library ($1,029,655 for 1978-79); the support of the Bridwells for the Perkins Library at Southern Methodist University; the $10 million in private donations for the new Dallas Public Library building; the gifts accompanying the transfer of the American Geographical Society Library to the University of Wisconsin at Milwaukee; the extensive fund-raising activities undertaken by three land-grant universities (Auburn, Iowa State, and Texas A&M); the significant gifts to bring the Hartford Theological Seminary Library to Emory University (rumored to be close to $3 million); contributions toward the Stanford University Library building; and the capital campaigns of the American Antiquarian Society, the Folger Shakespeare Library, and the Newberry Library.

In a very perceptive article, "The Ivory Tower in the Arena — Research Libraries and Public Outreach," in the January 1979 *Wilson Library Bulletin,* O.B. Hardison, Jr., argues that the need for research libraries to justify their existence in the marketplace has been a healthy development.[5] Their staffs have been forced to come down from the ivory tower and sell the library's mission to the general public. In noting that his own library once existed on endowment income alone, Dr. Hardison points out that, of the Folger Library's 1979 budget of $2.6 million, only $1.1 million, or about 40 percent, came from endowment.

In the 1978 *Annual Report of the Library Company of Philadelphia,* that inveterate critic of librarians and strange new bibliothecal views, Edwin Wolf II, decries this new emphasis on the marketplace with the selling of ties and tee-shirts and the use of other gimmicky money-raising schemes.[6] Yet Wolf's own aggressive efforts at seeking financial support resulted in that musty library again becoming a useful scholarly resource in the last decade. If I were a betting man, I'd place my bets on Dr. Hardison.

One can understand the nostalgia for the ivory tower or for the local reading room as a place of tranquility, and the shrinking from that kind of public relations that has made West Virginia State Librarian Fred Glazer the P.T. Barnum of the modern library world. But is it so foreign to our historical antecedents to expect librarians to understand their basic function, to be able to articulate that mission to their constituents, and to encourage their support, either through the political process or through fund raising? I suggest that what may be lacking is imagination and willingness to commit the time needed to explain the library's cause to the public. Wringing our

TABLE 3. Institutions Receiving Three or More Grants During 1969-79, by Amount (in Thousands of Dollars)*

Institution	1969	1970	1971	1972	1973	1974	1975	1976	1977	1978	1979
Davidson College	585	305		230		300					
Duke University	1525		1245 (2)		1500						
Harvard University	1000	500				1430	1000			650	
Pierpont Morgan Library		1249		670					1175 (3)		
Princeton University	300	1000	1000		1125						
Council on Library Resources			5000			6000					
New York Public Library				1646 (3)	1506 (2)	1500 (2)	625	1000	1205 (3)	2000 (3)	
University of Chicago			900 (2)	1000	575 (2)		350				
Center for Research Libraries			247	450	850 (2)						
Stanford University					348		1348 (2)		2267 (3)		
Research Libraries Group									750	750	2600 (5)

* Numbers in parentheses indicate number of grants made that year.

hands and wishing for a more tranquil era seems unlikely to assure libraries of the financial resources they need. On the other hand, I would like to explode a few myths which may stand in the way of the search for additional resources for libraries.

The first is the myth that citizens generally are uninterested in libraries. There is abundant evidence that support for libraries is strong and only awaits mobilization. The White House conference with all the turmoil it has caused, seems at least to have awakened citizens in many states to the value of libraries and the need for better support. But it is also clear that citizens have their own ideas about future library resources and services. One consequence of citizen participation will be their insistence that their views be taken seriously. That is no less true of donors to libraries or of those who encourage donations to libraries.

An example of citizen support is the New York Public Library (NYPL) which has rallied the NEH, the Vincent Astor Foundation, and others to keep that great cultural institution open. The NEH has awarded over $7 million to the NYPL, and the federal sums have been matched with $12 million in donations. Thanks to the Vincent Astor Foundation's support, the number of donations to the library has increased from 3000 in the early 1970s to almost 40,000 today. In North Carolina the construction of new public libraries and the expansion of school libraries owe much to the dedicated work of volunteers who carry the library's story to the local and state officials who must provide the funds for their continuing operation.

A second myth is that raising money is the only contribution one can make to a library. Raising money is important, and having some good accountants and lawyers among one's friends is a decided plus for any librarian, yet I remember that Guy Garrison's Ph.D. dissertation, a study of the bond referenda for the Seattle Public Library, indicated that the bond issue passed only after the labor unions and other neglected citizen groups were persuaded to support it.[7] We often overlook the fact that there are citizens — other than those in the League of Women Voters, the garden clubs, or the professional people in town — who have an interest in the library and will actively support its programs if convinced of the need.

The third myth is that it's easy to raise money. Whether local voters, the county court, the state legislature, or private donors are involved, it is *not* easy to raise money. One must be willing to commit time and energy to such efforts as an ongoing activity. Many university libraries are now adding their own development officers. Our neighbor, the Duke University Library, has done so and has set as a goal the raising of $750,000 annually through gifts and grants to the library. Particularly with government agencies and foundations, gift giving has been raised to an art, if not a science, and the library with the best chance of obtaining those funds will be the one which can write a proposal designed to fit the purposes of that particular organization.

Fourth, there is the myth that all libraries can raise money equally well. Much depends upon the institutional context in which the library functions. Clearly, it is easier to raise money for libraries in older, distinguished colleges and universities than in newer ones. It's also easier if the library has a well-identified constituency, such as Brandeis University's National Women's Committee, which has annually raised funds for that library since 1948 through a nationwide book sale in about 125 cities. Somewhat similar is the nine-year-old book sale of the Friends of the Chapel Hill Public Library, which this year sold approximately 15,000 books for a net total of more than $10,000 for the library book fund. This small public library is fortunate to operate in an "intellectually dense" community. Many books sold each year have appeared in previous sales and are passed from one family to another, to the enrichment of the library. Other communities are not so book-rich. Some communities have immense civic pride, even a large city like Houston, and this can often be used for the benefit of newer libraries. However, one should not appear before a subcommittee of the chamber of commerce, as one librarian did, and talk about a cookie sale. Rather, one should not hesitate to say quite candidly what the needs of the library are. Modesty about library needs in front of individuals who spend millions of dollars a year on other causes is not necessarily the best policy.

Understanding what one must ask for from a particular group or individual is an important part of raising funds. After I had been at University of North Carolina a while, I wrote my friend Henry Rockwell and asked for a modest gift for the library school. Typical of Henry's behavior when he didn't want to do something, he did not respond at all. Later, when my wife and I were attending a reception at the University of Houston, Henry remarked, "That was quite a letter you wrote me . . . but you didn't ask for enough." My comeback was, "Henry, I'll take care of that immediately." A year or so after that, Henry did respond, to the amusement of my Houston friends, by announcing a gift to University of North Carolina during a luncheon meeting of the University of Houston Friends Advisory Council when I was present!

What of the future? My own impression is that all librarians — of whatever type — are going to have to become more involved in the life of their communities if they are to receive the support needed to make their libraries more than a sleepy place for persons who can't earn their livelihood by more productive means. That will be tougher in the future because many organizations will be competing for the same dollars. No mail truck passes my door these days without one or two appeals for contributions to worthy causes or for votes on specific issues. The inflation rate has not only surpassed all expectations, but the end is scarcely in sight. And as for those of us in fields generally concerned with education, the public is increasingly skeptical that we know what we are doing, or that we do whatever it is we claim to do well. I see this as a challenge to the friends of libraries and to the librarians whom they support.

Marian Orgain, at the ALA Conference in Dallas last summer, pointed out that old donors are dying off and the newer generation seems less interested in doing things for others. I'm not sure this is true, but the times may well call for different approaches. The donor of small gifts has always been important, for he or she represents a group of well-educated individuals for whom libraries have the greatest appeal. Such donors often provide books or book funds out of all proportion to their means. They do so because books have meaning for them, and they want to share their intellectual heritage with others who will appreciate these resources and use them for their own personal and professional enrichment.

Yet I could not help being reminded of Ms. Orgain's comments one Friday morning, when CBS News announced that Mr. Robert Woodruff, long-time friend of Emory University, had just bestowed upon that institution 1 million shares of Coca-Cola stock worth approximately $100 million. This princely gift follows others made by him over the years, and one can well understand why the research library at Emory bears Mr. Woodruff's name. Moreover, last year the media revealed that Mr. Woodruff had given Atlanta University $10 million for a new library building. Is this Coca-Cola millionaire one link in a continuing saga of support for education and libraries, or is he, at ninety, one of the last of a group of wealthy benefactors whose like we shall not see again? No one can be sure. What we can be sure of, however, is that libraries will continue to need the support of friends, for I agree with Mrs. Fredrica Gross Dudley, one of the long-time friends of the University of Houston Libraries, who responded to a reception in her honor several years ago with these words: "A university without adequate libraries is one in name only. This conviction is the basis for my profound interest in the University of Houston Libraries. What could be more joyous or rewarding than the knowledge that one has helped, even in a small way, to make the stream of consciousness more dear? This is the rich heritage of all who found or help to build college libraries."

NOTES

1. Babb, James T. "The Yale University Library," *Library Trends* 15:206, Oct. 1966.
2. Querfield, Sara, ed. *Report of the University Librarian, July 1977–June 1978* (Bulletin of Yale University, series 75, no. 1). New Haven, Conn., Yale University, Jan. 1, 1979, p. 31.
3. Kaser, David. "The Golden Touch; or the Gentle Art of Raising Money," *Stechert-Hafner Book News* 19:109-11, May 1965.
4. Prentice, Ann E. "Government Funding." *In* Patricia S. Breivik and E. Gibson Burr, eds. *Funding Alternatives for Libraries.* Chicago, ALA, 1979, pp. 79-93. *See also* Eaton, Andrew J. "Fund Raising for University Libraries." *In* ibid., pp. 129-41.
5. Hardison, O.B., Jr. "The Ivory Tower in the Arena — Research Libraries and Public Outreach," *Wilson Library Bulletin* 53:384-91, Jan. 1979.
6. Library Company of Philadelphia. *Annual Report for the Year 1978.* Philadelphia, 1979.
7. Garrison, Guy G. "Voting Behavior on Public Library Bond Issues: An Analysis of Three Elections in Seattle, Washington, 1950-1956." Ph.D. diss., University of Illinois, 1960.

ADDITIONAL REFERENCES

Gwyn, Ann, et al. "Friends of the Library," *College & Research Libraries* 36:272-82, July 1975.
Hopp, Ralph H. "Private and Industrial Funds for University Libraries," *College & Research Libraries* 23:509-13, Nov. 1962.
Kaser, David. "Outside Funding of Academic Libraries," *Library Trends* 11:353-61, April 1963.
Leatherbury, Maurice C., and Lyders, Richard A. "Friends of the Library Groups in Health Sciences Libraries," *Bulletin of the Medical Library Association* 66:315-18, July 1978.
Lynden, Frederick C. "External Fund Raising for Book Funds — A CLR Fellowship Report. *In* Association of Research Libraries. Office of University Library Management Studies. Systems and Procedures Exchange Center. *SPEC Kit 48: External Fund Raising in ARL Libraries.* Oct. 1978.

SCOTT BENNETT

Library Friends: A Theoretical History

There may at first appear to be a world of difference between the Ambrosiana Library, founded in Milan in 1609 to preserve Renaissance learning, and the St. Joseph Public Library, founded in 1934 to serve an Illinois farm community fifty miles from Allerton Park. Great as the differences are, these libraries have one thing in common — the one thing, in fact, that most libraries share. They have attracted the support of private benefactors. These two libraries owe their very existence to such benefactors, to the vision and zeal of Cardinal Federigo Borromeo on the one hand, and of the St. Joseph Women's Club on the other. Private support of this sort has played a key role throughout the history of libraries. Excavations of some pre-Alexandrian libraries have uncovered names of donors inscribed on their walls; Oxford's magnificent Bodleian began with the gift of Sir Thomas Bodley; the New York Public Library was built first on its three great private foundations and then expanded throughout the city with Carnegie-built buildings; for most of us the names Clements, Folger, Huntington, and Lilly are first of all the names of library benefactors. It is well to remember these few examples, and to remember that the St. Joseph Public Library was first supported by the Women's Club and that its present building and an endowment providing a substantial part of its operating funds were the gift of Maude Davis as recently as 1955.[1] These things remind us that the map of libraries in the United States was very largely laid down through private gifts.[2] The centuries-long history of these gifts, however they were given and whatever they were called, is the history of library friends.[3]

The purpose of any history is to free us from the chance operation of memory, to give structure and force to what we remember. I wish I could report that there exists a formal history of library friends and private benefactions that preserves the record of what has been accomplished. But there is no such history, even though the subject is a rich one. That is the reason for the title of this essay: its subject does not exist, but needs to be called into existence. To help bring that about and to help give point to the deliberations of this conference, three things are needed. We must recognize the key events of the mid-nineteenth century that have shaped library development since then; we must understand why we talk about library benefactors and friends as having a theoretical rather than an actual history; and finally, we must recognize what the issues are in this history and why it is important that our history become a vital force in shaping what we do. This discussion is confined to the history of English and American libraries because that is what I know and because their history presents some instructive contrasts.

Looking back to the nineteenth century, we must remember that before 1850 there was only a small handful of libraries in the English-speaking world that could properly be called "public." Libraries 130 years ago were primarily either profit-making commercial operations, an offshoot of bookselling, or cooperative ventures altogether dependent on private support. These last might be earnest ventures with distinguished histories, like Franklin's Library Company of Philadelphia, or they might be more club-like operations, such as the London Library. Be that as it may, they were unmistakably private institutions. And just as unmistakably, there was no alternative provision of public access to books and information.

It was therefore a fundamental change in pattern when public, tax-supported libraries began to develop in several mid-nineteenth-century New England communities and when, on the old side of the Atlantic, an act of Parliament empowered English towns to create public libraries. The change appears more dramatic in England because there it was a matter of national debate and legislation. One opponent of Ewart's 1850 public library bill identified the key issue by taking a stand, as he said, "against the substitution of the compulsory for the voluntary principle in all matters of education."[4] Exactly so: in creating public, tax-supported libraries, Ewart's bill was to transform altogether the role of voluntary support. Where before the benefactor, be it a single person or a corporate group, brought the library into existence and guided its development, now the benefactor had only a complementary and a secondary role to play. Libraries were now created as a matter of public deliberation (often after a vote of taxpayers), and library operations were a matter of public policy, controlled by officers answerable to the public. Of course lines were not drawn this sharply at first, and private benefactors were often influential in moving public opinion. But it was clear as the nineteenth century came to a close that the question for private benefactors had become how to play a supporting rather than a leading role in library development, how to relate their activities to the dominant activities of the state. It is this dramatic shift in roles for friends of libraries that lies at the heart of the distinction between voluntary and compulsory principles of action.

Although legislation changed the ground rules for private supporters of libraries, that legislation also quite explicitly provided for and depended on voluntary action. The English law of 1850 granted public provision for library buildings and operating costs only. The provision of books, magazines, and newspapers — the heart of the matter — was explicitly reserved to

private benefaction. The New Hampshire act of 1849 empowered libraries to receive, hold, and dispose of gifts and bequests; and the very occasion for the Massachusetts library law of 1851 was a private gift to establish a public library in Wayland.[5] The point to emphasize is that even where private initiative led the way, it did so now with careful regard toward public policy and law. The specific division of responsibilities first established — private provision of books and public provision of buildings — quickly proved unworkable. In fact, it was dramatically reversed in the program of that most famous and openhanded of all library benefactors, Andrew Carnegie.[6] The $56 million that Carnegie gave to libraries went for buildings only, and only where local authorities agreed to use tax revenues to fill those buildings with reading material and to maintain services to readers. Carnegie firmly believed in the principle of matching funds; he unhesitatingly asserted that his gifts were meant to prime the public pump. Carnegie's gifts to public libraries are cumulatively the most spectacular ever made, and their number and wide geographical spread only drive home the fact that what private benefactors did now was largely conditioned by the state of public law and policy. The role of the private supporter of libraries is to complement that policy, to prompt widespread adoption of it, and to enhance its effectiveness when adopted. This pattern was first established 130 years ago and is still very much with us.

Many of the speakers opposed to Ewart's 1850 public library bill wanted to preserve the older pattern, in which private initiative was dominant. That view did not prevail then — it lost by only seventeen votes — nor has it prospered since. For of course the public provision of libraries is but part of a much larger movement in modern history, in which the state has taken up more and more of the responsibilities for health, education, and welfare that were before left to private benefactors.[7] Problems of industrialization and urbanization simply overwhelmed private action and required concerted public remedies; the result has been the welfare state. However one views this central development in modern history, it is clear that libraries have participated in it. We now think of libraries as primarily public institutions and of tax funds as their "natural" source of support. We now talk about library friends as providing the "margin of excellence." No one doubts that this is a vital function, but there is also no doubt that it has become a marginal one in relation to public provision.

The takeover of the John Rylands Library by the University of Manchester in England and the struggle of the Folger Library in this country to retain its independent status illustrate how marginal private benefaction can become. Public provision has become so dominant in England that a library friends group is something that now has to be explained there, even to librarians and library historians. Except for a remnant Friends of the National Libraries, there is little interest in or understanding of private support for public libraries in England.[8] I mention this to illustrate how dominant public provision has become, but also to insist that there is nothing inevitable about it. For in the United States we are experiencing a renaissance of private support for libraries, as in the 1930s when libraries were threatened by hard times much as they are now. The sharp contrasts between the condition of private library support in the two countries suggest that though we are both caught up in the main movement of modern history, we still have it in our power to shape our own responses to it. We cannot suspend this most potent movement in modern history or free ourselves from its influence; but we can work out a distinctive and critically important role for library friends within the broader movement of events — if we choose to do so.

I have so far argued that private supporters of libraries can still have a catalytic role in the development of libraries, but that the creation of public libraries in the mid-nineteenth century altered in fundamental and probably irrevocable ways the nature of that role. This change in the basic chemistry of library support is the fundamental fact in the history of library friends. What then are the other facts?

While there are many more instances of the key importance of private support in the creation and development of libraries, there is no better account of the structure of events in our history. The problem is that no history of library friends exists. We do not have a detailed or instructive account of friends activities, of why they prosper or fail, of what roles private benefactors play at different times in the history of the libraries they support. There are any number of facts about the formation of friends groups in the 1920s and 1930s, about how tax laws in Michigan or the federal tax code have helped to stimulate library support, about how much money the Friends of the Library of Columbia University raised between 1950 and 1970, or even about the per capita amount of library gifts in several southwestern states between 1930 and 1940 (in Texas it was just over $0.29).[9] We have facts like these, but no one has built from them a coherent history of library benefaction. We can go beyond these established facts to speculate that the 1930s saw an important shift in this country from individual to corporately organized library support. We might also speculate that the differences between England and the United States reflect different tax laws and basic differences in attitudes toward state and individual action. But if we want to penetrate such hopelessly broad generalizations, if we want to find out more particularly why library benefaction has largely disappeared in England or why it thrives in this country, we cannot do what we would normally do: go confidently to our libraries to get the answer. The answer — our own history — simply does not exist.

There are several reasons why even the outlines of the history of library benefaction are so indistinct. One is that most of the published record focuses on local and nonrecurring events. The literature of library friends is highly discontinuous. Another reason is that the archival records of friends activities do not survive well. If saved at all, these documents are often entangled in the papers of individuals or of larger organizations — because friends activities are themselves so entangled. This is true, for instance, of the Carnegie papers, though in this case the records of Carnegie's library activities have received separate analysis. Another exception is the record of the Detroit Public Library Friends; a large body of papers representing many years of activity survive. The American Library Association's involvement with friends activities is documented in the archives of ALA housed at the University of Illinois at Urbana-Champaign.[10] But it is the exceptions that we know; the rule is that the records of private support for most libraries do not survive or are difficult to isolate among other library records. It may be that we have grown careless of the record of friends groups because their activities are so familiar to us, because we see nothing extraordinary in them. If this is so, we should recall the walls of those pre-Alexandrian libraries or learn a lesson from Sir Thomas Bodley, who meticulously recorded in his own hand all the gifts to his new library in Oxford. He would entrust this task to no one else, and his ledger was kept near the door for all to see.[11]

The paucity of the existing record results most of all from the failure of friends to care about their own history. Friends organizations are usually goal-oriented and are vitalized by strong but intermittent leadership. They are essentially forward-looking organizations focused on present challenges and tomorrow's activities. One result of this is that friends groups wax and wane quite dramatically. The Friends of the Library of Columbia University, for instance, was founded by mathematician David Eugene Smith in 1928 and flourished until the mid-1930s, when ill health forced Smith to withdraw. The organization simply died in 1938 and had to be recreated altogether in 1951 under the leadership of Mark Van Doren and August Hecksher.[12] The organizational discontinuity of such strong friends groups as Columbia's typifies the general failure of library friends to root themselves firmly in their own past. Any friends group that neglects its history may have to repeat it, even to the point of having to rebuild itself altogether. History is, after all, a mode of self-consciousness. If we do not know our own past, it will be all the more difficult to persuade anyone — either ourselves or those we wish to join us — that we can play an important role in the development of libraries.

We have only a theoretical history of library friends because the printed record of such benefaction is so disjointed, because archival records do not survive, and — most importantly — because we ourselves do not much value our past. Some may feel that that is as it should be, that library giving is by nature local and discontinuous, and that what matters in organizing the library's support is the present and immediate future, not the past. I believe otherwise and would like to close this paper by doing two things. I would like to identify three key issues in the history of library benefaction and suggest why it is important that we take up these issues.

The first and most basic issue is the way private support marks our perception of the needs and purposes of public libraries. We know, for instance, that the most visible activity of private benefactors has been the provision of buildings — the great Brown Library in Liverpool, opened in 1860, and the John F. Kennedy Library, opened in Boston just recently, are examples that stand at either end of our history. These buildings embody in stone and mortar the sometimes grand and always instructive perceptions held by their sponsors of what libraries should be and how they should serve the community in which they are placed. This perception of need and function is also embodied in many other friends activities, activities that more directly reflect the critical balance struck between the public and private provision of library needs, and the way that balance changes as perceptions change. The history of the Friends of the University of North Carolina Library makes this clear. As recently as 1949 the friends of that library were supporting it with gifts that exceeded the value of the entire state appropriations for books, serials, and binding. In 1953 care was taken not to publish the value of friends support lest legislators feel that those gifts were an adequate substitute for public appropriations. It was only in 1962 that state appropriations reached a level that enabled the Friends of the University of North Carolina Library to attend to other than the basic needs of the library.[13] The issue here is the perception of need. And though the University of North Carolina Library may be an unusual case, libraries — along with hospitals, medical research, and some parts of higher education — have probably been the institutions least thoroughly swept into the modern state's assumption of responsibility for health, education, and welfare. For that reason, these institutions reflect most directly the balances that are still being struck between the voluntary and compulsory principles of action for meeting public needs — principles clearly identified in the parliamentary debate over Ewart's bill in 1850.

Closely related to the perception of need is the issue of how that perception was implemented. This is a question of how resources were used, of how well the balance between public and private provision actually served libraries, of how that balance helped to shape the administration of libraries. The best-known case in point is the impact of Carnegie gifts on the development of both individual libraries and libraries generally. As eager as many communities were to secure a free library building, not a few of them were unwilling or unable to meet the concomitant obligation to provide books and operating costs with public funds. The halfpenny rate in England and meager tax revenues in many North American towns left libraries with only enough money to maintain their new buildings, but not to stock them with books or pay for an adequate library staff. Private gifts thus brought many libraries into existence that then limped on decade after decade with decidedly inadequate public support. This was most noticeable in communities with a population too small to provide an adequate tax base, however enthusiastic that population might be about its library.[14] Small, inefficiently operated units have long burdened the development of library services in this country and in England. The administrative mesh — or lack of it — between public and private resources is a central and recurrent issue that embraces much more than the provision of buildings. Any librarian who has had to deal with gift books knows the danger such gifts pose of consuming inordinate amounts of time and diplomacy, and of distorting library collections with material of marginal utility.[15] These are problems in the management of private gifts that led one administrator writing about library friends to title his essay "That Splendid Headache."[16]

Finally and perhaps most interestingly, there is the issue of motives. American library historians have vigorously debated the motives behind the individual initiative and private support that so decisively helped to launch the public library movement.[17] Was the movement an altruistic expression of the American dream of self-help and independence, or was it prompted by a fear of working-class restiveness that might be controlled by the public provision of self-education and "safe" reading? Carnegie's gifts — especially of the library at Homestead — posed sticky questions for the labor movement and the American left. They could hardly forget the working conditions in Carnegie plants when listening to the Scotsman open a new library or explain his "Gospel of Wealth." In the control and distribution of wealth, questions of motive are always important and seem easier to answer when they are comfortably remote in time. Nearer to hand they become more complex — as in, for instance, the rationale behind the tax benefits accorded to gifts to charities and nonprofit organizations. At issue here, as well as in the founding of the Boston Public Library or Carnegie's provision of libraries, is the transformation of private wealth into public wealth. But note the all-important fact that this transformation takes place to a significant degree outside the mechanism of taxation, legislation, and public determination of policy that controls most of the appropriation of private wealth for the public good. Almost everyone will agree that private benefaction does much good, though it produces many tax dodges and is subject to other abuses. Problems in securing the benefits of private giving without the abuses arise because our motives are usually so thoroughly mixed. It is this basic aspect of human nature that shapes the issues in the transformation of private wealth into public wealth, and makes the history of that transformation so interesting.

These then are the three issues that would emerge first and most strongly if we were to create an actual rather than a theoretical history of library friends. Let me close by indicating briefly the benefits we might realize by a more careful investigation of that history. The first benefit would be for library friends themselves. We must have a history; we must be conscious of our past if we are to be vitally important to libraries now and in the future. If we cannot say where we have been, where we are now, and where we want to go, we may find ourselves altogether out of the picture. I believe that has already happened in England. There are many reasons for that, including the tax structure and pervasive attitudes about the proper sphere of government action. But none of these things "just happens." Events now are driven by the earlier events, and we must understand how this occurs if we are to avoid being altogether driven by them ourselves. In this sense, understanding our history is a matter of survival for library friends. Working out our history would also yield benefits to the libraries we support. Friends provide one focus for the definition of aspirations in libraries and library service. These aspirations may be good, bad, or debatable ones, but they give voice to what we want our libraries to be. And they are formed by people deeply attached to libraries but not professionally responsible for them. To understand this role of friends and to see how their aspirations have taken shape and been managed in the past is to give human form and substance to our history, as well as to the statistics of library performance on which we increasingly depend in deciding policy. Library friends offer us one means (but certainly not the only one) for understanding the humanity of actual library users. Finally, there is a benefit to us all in the creation of a history of library benefaction. It is the benefit of broader comprehension and wiser living that informs all history as a humanistic study. In the case of library benefaction, what we are studying is the paradigm of a common experience in modern life. It is the juxtaposition of private and public life, the establishment through private volunteer action of public communities of interest. The drive begun 130 years ago in the English-speaking world to replace private, commercially based, and exclusive collections of books with public libraries and free access to knowledge is a movement from fragmentation and isolation toward the creation of a common cause. Matthew Arnold's distinction between culture and anarchy may be fruitfully applied here, as it can in so many other areas. Arnold lamented the anarchy of simply "doing as one likes" with one's own property.[18] He understood what so many of our Victorian forebears — including that great robber baron, Andrew Carnegie — understood: that wealth is essentially a public thing, to be used for the public good. They in their imperfect way, and we in ours, are concerned with the transformation of private goods into public ones, with the creation of the commonwealth. This is the triumph of culture over anarchy. These are highly colored words, but they do justice to that triumph of human nature of which the history of library benefaction is a part.

NOTES

1. *See* Smalling, Donna. *St. Joseph, Illinois: 1972 Centennial.* n.p., 1972, pp. 130-31.

2. Butler, Pierce. "The Dentition of *Equus Donatus*," *Library Quarterly* 1:204, April 1931.

3. I am indebted to the University of Illinois Library for its support, and to Jeannette Cook for her invaluable help in the preparation of this paper.

4. Palmer, Roundell. *In* Great Britain. Parliament. "Public Libraries and Museums Bills," *Hansard's Parliamentary Debates*, 3d ser., vol. 109, col. 848, 1850.

5. Summary accounts of early library legislation appear *in* Thomas Kelly. *A History of Public Libraries in Great Britain 1845-1965.* London, Library Association, 1973, pp. 3-15; and *in* Jesse H. Shera. *Foundations of the Public Library: The Origins of the Public Library Movement in New England, 1629-1855.* Chicago, University of Chicago Press, 1949, pp. 156-99.

6. Carnegie's support of American libraries is fully chronicled *in* George S. Bobinski. *Carnegie Libraries: Their History and Impact on American Public Library Development.* Chicago, ALA, 1969. The best account of Carnegie's British library benefactions is found *in* James G. Ollé. "Andrew Carnegie: The Unloved Benefactor," *Library World* 70:255-62, April 1969.

7. The changing balance between private benefaction and state action is masterfully chronicled *in* David E. Owen. *English Philanthropy 1660-1960.* Cambridge, Mass., Harvard University Press, 1964. This writer knows no comparable study of American philanthropy.

8. *See* Blakeney, T.S. "The Friends of the National Libraries," *Private Library* (2d ser.) 8:120-24, Autumn 1975; and Day, Alan. "Friends of the National Libraries," *New Library World* 77:219-21, Nov. 1976.

9. *See* Vance, Eleanor G. "Libraries Find New Friends," *Saturday Review* 35:9-10+, July 5, 1952; Culver, Essae M., and Gittinger, Nantelle M. "A History of the Citizens' Library Movement," *Bulletin of the Louisiana Library Association* 17:18-23, Winter 1954; Scupholm, Paul T. "The Library's Friends — Their Responsibility to the Community . . . and the Library! !" *Michigan Librarian* 41:11-12, Spring 1975; Boyer, Joseph A. "Philanthropy and High Taxes," *ALA Bulletin* 32:427-30, July 1938; "Activities of the Friends," *Columbia Library Columns* 21:46, Nov. 1971; and Carlson, William H. "Library Philanthropy in the Southwest." *In* Southwestern Library Association. *Tenth Biennial Conference: Papers and Proceedings.* n.p., 1940, pp. 84-93.

10. The pertinent record series in the ALA Archives are 18/1/26 and 27/14/3-7.

The location of other library friends documentation is recorded *in* "National Catalog of Sources for the History of Librarianship," a computer printout from a data base maintained by the University of Illinois Archives.

11. "Sir Thomas Bodley on Donors and Donations," *Dartmouth College Library Bulletin* 2:128-31, March 1937.

12. Hyde, Mary C. "History of Library Friends and the Phoenix Story of Columbia," *Columbia Library Columns* 20:3, 12-13, May 1971. The general organizational instability of friends groups is observed *in* Oliver Garceau. *The Public Library in the Political Process: A Report of the Public Library Inquiry.* New York, Columbia University Press, 1949, p. 119.

13. Turner, Barbara L. "The Friends of the University of North Carolina Library, 1932-1962." Master's thesis, University of North Carolina, 1965, pp. 26, 41, 33.

14. *See* Bobinski, op. cit., pp. 96-102, 152-53; Munn, Ralph. "Hindsight on the Gifts of Carnegie . . . ," *Library Journal* 76:1968-69, Dec. 1, 1951; and Ollé, op. cit., pp. 258-62.

15. *See* Butler, op. cit., pp. 207-11.

16. Healey, James S. "That Splendid Headache," *Library Journal* 87:2990-93, Sept. 15, 1962.

17. For a guide to this debate, *see* Harris, Michael H., and Davis, Donald G., Jr. *American Library History: A Bibliography.* Austin, University of Texas Press, 1978, pp. 59-60.

18. Arnold, Matthew. *Culture and Anarchy: An Essay in Political and Social Criticism.* London, Smith, Elder, 1869, pp. 51-92.

SANDY DOLNICK

The Present State of Library Friends

The Friends of Libraries Committee of the Public Relations Section of the Library Administration and Management Association (LAMA), as should be well known by now, has given birth to a new group called Friends of Libraries U.S.A. Some of the reasons which led to this development should be singled out. The first is the healthy state of friends of libraries today: there are at least 2000 groups, with a membership which has been conservatively estimated at one-half million members. The second is the directory which lists these groups.[1] The third is a book of essays on library friends groups, scheduled for publication in November 1980, complementing the book by Sarah Wallace issued in 1962.[2] Another strong influence is the newsletter, called *Friends of the Library National Notebook.*[3] Originally subsidized by LAMA, the newsletter was begun with the hope that 400 subscribers would be enlisted to cover expenses. Today we have 700; in the future the newsletter will be available only to the members of Friends of Libraries U.S.A.

As editor of the book of essays and the newsletter, and president of the new organization, I would like to share some observations by way of describing the present state of our library friends groups. The basis of this paper involves my own observations, as well as a survey conducted in connection with the forthcoming book. For this survey, over 700 groups were selected at random from public and academic libraries; we had a 46 percent response rate. The following data, gathered in 1977-78, are probably still valid:

90 percent of the responses were from public libraries.
31 percent of these public libraries served a population of between 25,000 and 100,000.
6 percent of them served a population of more than 500,000.
Of the groups surveyed, 47 percent of the libraries had collections of less than 100,000 volumes.
46 percent of the respondents represented libraries with budgets of less than $500,000.
Unions were not a factor in most of the libraries.
Most of the groups were organized after 1950.

Most of the groups had fewer than 200 members.

Once formed, most groups have been continually active.

Most are exempt from federal and state taxes.

Paid help is uncommon for all but the largest groups.

Most groups prefer not to use the word *lobby,* but nevertheless are strong advocates of their library.

Library staff members, usually the library director, are almost always involved with successful groups.

Most states do not have a state group to which the group could belong.

Most groups felt the need for a national organization.

It is important to keep this profile in mind when talking about friends of libraries. If this survey is valid, most groups exist in relatively small towns or colleges. This enhances their scope considerably, since friends can play a much more important part in the life of a small community than in a large one.

It is overwhelming to consider the variety of activities undertaken by friends. I would like to give a sampling of some that have come to my attention. Two types of programs have been used historically to bring library friends groups to the attention of the public: the book-and-author program and the book sale. The book sale can be a continuing event or it may be held at given intervals throughout the year. It can be made up of library discards, or of contributions from citizens. It is important not only because it fosters goodwill in the community (who can resist a bargain?), but also because it needs people to organize it, thus providing a means of member involvement. It can also bring in new members, who are drawn to the sale and want to enjoy the privilege of a members-only preview. Libraries are much more than collections of books, but library friends are still attracted by that image. Ours may be among the last few generations to enjoy the search through a card file or the leisurely perusal of the stacks, but the tangible feeling of a book in hand has a powerful emotional appeal to friends of libraries. The elusive spirit of a creative person is one of the attractions of the book-and-author program. What kind of person writes your favorite type of fiction or history? Members may be shy in speaking directly to the author, but the appeal of seeing and hearing an author is still a powerful one. Local or imported, the writer may not be a very good speaker, but will still have an intangible aura.

These two types of programs, book-and-author programs and book sales, may be best for fund raising because of their association with books. The books can be priced so that anyone can afford to buy; or the prices may exceed fair market value, as in an antiquarian book sale of donated items, so that more money is raised.

Other types of book-related programs involve book production or illustration. Book review programs are popular, involving either a panel discussing a topic suggested by books, or a review of a specific book by a single person. Book discussion groups are also popular. Another money-making venture is a book fair, in which new books are sold at regular prices, with the group getting some percentage of the sales.

Certainly, library friends are anxious to show off their libraries and the mechanisms, new and old, that are a part of it. These programs are appropriate any time of year, not just during National Library Week. They can range from sessions on how to use the library to demonstrations of new equipment or displays of part of the library collection, such as new books, rare books, current or nostalgic films, videotapes, paintings, travel information — the list is as extensive as the resources of a library.

Programs of a social nature are a means of bringing other members of the community into the library group, not only through enlarging membership, but also through enhancing the group's stature in the community as it relates more meaningfully to other groups. For those people who are afraid they do not read enough or are not smart enough to be a friend of the library, such programs are a good way of showing the diversity of the library's community.

Many groups have found that introducing new paintings for rent, purchase, or just for show brings in a new type of friend, willing to help with display and to find artists to show their work. The same is true of concert series. There is generally space available for both types of activity at a library, and the surroundings are conducive to the enjoyment of art, music and books. Programs which mix the arts are especially popular in academic libraries.

Cosponsorship of a program with another group is an excellent way to enlarge the scope of your group. The League of Women Voters often needs help with a "Candidates Night." The local historical or genealogical society, familiar with area history records, is often willing to demonstrate the work involved in tracing a family tree. Cosponsorship of a theater or symphony night has raised funds for libraries, providing a pleasant evening as well. One must remember that there is nothing wrong with such fun. Too serious an image eliminates a large part of the population from your group's potential support. Also, remember various ethnic groups when planning your year's programs. Many friends groups accent ethnic heritage during the holiday season, but a national holiday of another country might also be appropriate for celebration.

Craft programs are always popular and can provide for your group a core of helpers known to be good with their hands, industrious, and able to carry on long-term projects. Sometimes these same people can be prevailed upon to address envelopes or to do telephoning; a reception can show off their finished projects.

Consumer advocacy and legal counsel, tax and estate planning, and real estate and stock investment programs bring in different groups and provide a very real service. The books in the library on these subjects can be shown and coffee served.

Social evenings set in the library building give a different slant to what we see behind the bricks and mortar. "Supper in the stacks" was held in Manhasset, New York: volunteer chefs among the friends prepared and served their specialties and distributed their recipes. An ice cream social and a strawberry festival have been held in other localities. The Laura Ingalls Wilder Gingerbread Sociable, in Pomona, California, sounds delicious. The Bookfellows of Milwaukee held a tea dance in the rotunda of the central library building, celebrating the library's centennial and evoking the period of the 1920s.

Other groups have sponsored tours. Four academic library friends groups in California joined to visit a Folger Shakespeare Library exhibit in San Francisco. The Cleveland Friends as a group visited the Metropolitan Toronto Library. Other tours may not be book- or library-related. A tour of homes is as appropriate for a library friends group as for an art club, as is a trip to a neighboring town to see a museum or a show.

One of the most ambitious plans for a year's programs is sponsored by the Mount Lebanon Public Library Association near Pittsburgh. They require only a minimum donation of one dollar for membership and offer these numerous opportunities for fun, self-improvement and volunteer work:

Volunteer opportunities
Friends Reading Aloud program at the Baptist and Methodist Home
Homebound service delivery
Addressing envelopes for Friends
Being host or hostess at library programs
Staffing Friends' membership desk at library during annual drive
Participation on telephone committee
Delivering posters to local stores to advertise book sale
Helping sort books for sale

Learning opportunities
Genealogy study group
French, Spanish and German conversation groups
Informal book review group
Storytellers (a group which meets to learn about and practice storytelling)
Book discussion group
Art appreciation group

Local history project
Chess club
Backgammon club
Craft workshop

One cannot help but admire the enthusiasm of this friends group and congratulate its leaders in their success in involving its membership. It may not be advisable to plan so much in a larger community, where other groups might offer much the same types of opportunities, but if the Mount Lebanon Public Library ever needs citizen support, it will have a core group and half the battle won. Money helps, but it isn't everything; without friends to speak up for it, a library during a budget crunch has to start from scratch to find supporters.

Some librarians feel that friends are not as effective politically as a citizens committee formed for one specific purpose, for instance, to get a bond issue passed or to prevent closings of branches. I disagree. Friends can be whatever you want them to be, and within federally established guidelines, friends groups can set up separate committees to handle special programs and funds for political purposes.

But the days of "ladies who do nothing but pour tea and hold bake sales" is long past. There still are some, and treasure them if you are lucky enough to know them. But volunteerism is no longer something to fill time until the next bridge game. It is a commitment citizens make for a stronger community, important for our standard of living as we know it today and for the amenities we take for granted. Many enlightened businesses now support their workers in volunteer activities, even to the extent of loaning them to charities for special causes, or giving them time off to discharge volunteer duties. Community service is an important part of a person's resume, and libraries must learn to take advantage of this. Many businesses also make cash commitments to tax-exempt institutions, as the work of library friends in Detroit and Minneapolis will attest. It is in this climate of increased appreciation of volunteers, and of acknowledgment that friends are not something to pull out of a hat once a year to thank for their flower arrangements, that Friends of Libraries U.S.A. was born.

Undoubtedly, the specter of Proposition 13 has had a lot to do with the increased interest in friends. California, which has always had a strong friends organization, found that friends were there to pick up the pieces after the politicians left. In Los Angeles County alone, forty-two new friends organizations were started last year. Friends have always given time and money. And they responded to the crisis, as in Palos Verdes peninsula, where fifty volunteers check, maintain, and shelve the record collection, read the shelves weekly, clear the book drop daily, answer the phone, and help with children's programs. They are being taught to repair damaged books, sculptures and paintings. They will be used to run the audiovisual department, help with typing, maintain the local history room and picture file. They are freeing the professional librarian to do professional work, and not taking over the librarian's role, as so many fear.

Inquiries for materials on how to form a friends group come in regularly from librarians of small, large, academic, public, state, and system libraries. There has been something of a bandwagon feeling, for whatever reasons, and this past year was clearly the time to begin a national organization. Friends need to know more about each other, since in numbers there is strength. A network is needed to help encourage others to become friends. The public needs to be aware of friends groups and of the services they perform. The American Library Association has been most helpful in supporting this project, in the belief that citizen involvement is healthy and vital to the continuance of good library service. The timing of the White House conference may be just right, but special attention will be needed to assure that the friends momentum will not dissipate when the conference ends.

Friends of Libraries U.S.A. hopes to see individuals, groups, and libraries continue to work together, and to provide a necessary link in their communication. Please let us know what you're doing and how you are doing it. We also hope to be able to fill information gaps and to provide workshops on subjects of interest to friends. Our first effort will be a public relations kit containing television, radio and newspaper material for public service use, so as to enhance the friends' image from coast to coast. Many small groups lack the capabilities or expertise to produce these materials. We do not plan to raise funds for any purpose except our own expenses; our member groups are fighting their own fight for every dollar they raise, and it should rightly go to their libraries. For that reason, we have a sliding dues scale.

The board will seek a wide representation, geographically and by kind of library. Our first annual meeting will be held during the ALA conference in New York in summer 1980. You are cordially urged to join and to have your friends join.

In conclusion, and as a sample of our group efforts, it is useful to repeat the "Ten Commandments for Friends of Libraries." The list was compiled in part from my own experience, and in part from the 320 responses to our survey questionnaire. Certain elements repeated themselves; some are based on comments made because we promised anonymity; some come from librarians and some from friends. The rules should apply both to groups about to be formed and to those which encounter rough sailing:

Ten Commandments for Friends of Libraries
  1. The head librarian must want a friends group.

2. The library staff must be willing to work with the friends.
3. Those involved must be willing to make a commitment of time.
4. The library must make a commitment as to which of its resources may be used by the friends group (space, staff time, paper, artist, printing, phones, desks, etc.).
5. A core group of interested people must exist.
6. The authority to which the librarian is responsible (the trustees, the provost) should be aware of and in agreement with the need for a friends group.
7. Communication must be open among all groups concerned with library policy.
8. It is agreed that friends are not concerned with library policy.
9. The group must understand the role that it is expected to play.
10. It must be clear that the functions of the trustees and friends are separate.[4]

This is my prescription for a healthy group. The state of friends of library groups today *is* vital and healthy. One has the feeling that friends, having survived the period of passivity and having been tolerated in many instances as a necessary evil, have come to be accepted in the modern library and by their librarians as part of the community. As libraries increase their reliance on friends as a means of reaching the public, friends should continue to increase in effectiveness. As we begin the 1980s with a solid growth spurt, bolstered by the citizens involved in the White House conference and the framework of Friends of Libraries U.S.A., it is a pleasure to say that the state of friends of libraries has never been better. Indeed, its potential has just barely been explored.

NOTES

1. Dolnick, Sandy, comp. *Friends of the Library National Notebook: A Directory of Friends of Libraries Groups in the United States.* Chicago, ALA, Library Administration and Management Association, 1978.
2. _____, ed. *Friends of the Library Sourcebook.* Chicago, ALA, 1980. (In process.) *See also* Wallace, Sarah L., ed. *Friends of the Library: Organization and Activities.* Chicago, ALA, 1962.
3. *Friends of the Library National Notebook.* Sandy Dolnick, ed. Library Administration and Management Association, American Library Association, 50 E. Huron, Chicago, Ill. 60611. 1978- .
4. Dolnick, *Friends of the Library Sourcebook,* op. cit. (Reprinted with permission of publisher.)

ANNE J. MATHEWS

Library Friends and Regional Library Networks

The pre-White House Governor's Conferences on Library and Information Services have served to emphasize to all of us the importance of citizen input to — and interest in — libraries and library services. From around the country, reports of state conferences indicate that concerned citizens are banding together to form local, regional, and, in some places, state groups of lay people for the purpose of providing effective support for libraries. There is an excitement about libraries as a result of the pre-White House conferences. In a recent issue of *Library Journal,* we are reminded that "delegates are concerned citizens and have been preparing themselves for one year by reading, hearing, and thinking through thousands of resolutions, editorials, articles, etc."[1] This statement refers to Oklahoma White House conference delegates, but it applies to lay delegates from all fifty states.

However, not every concerned citizen is a White House conference delegate; many people who are involving themselves in statewide support groups represent local Friends of Libraries groups. Friends of libraries have been supporting their local libraries for many years. As Sandy Dolnick has so aptly pointed out, "All Friends of libraries are citizens. Therefore, all citizens are [prospective] Friends of Libraries."[2] Growing interest in friends activities at the state and national levels gives credence to the belief that citizens do care about libraries.

My personal association with a library friends group has given me an opportunity to see citizen involvement in action. Several years ago I was asked to join the Board of Managers of the Friends of the Denver Public Library. I am a library school professor, and as a professional, I do not have a vested interest in any one library. As a citizen, I have participated in concerned lay groups such as the League of Women Voters and a county-wide public school curriculum advisory committee. Therefore, I felt that the Denver Public Library's Friends board would provide me with an opportunity to work closely with lay people concerned about libraries. The amounts of time, energy, imagination, and hard work which these people have volunteered on behalf of the library are amazing. There have been legislative lunches, breakfasts, teas, cocktail parties, and tours of the library, and while not all of the city council members and state legislators have attended, the library's visibility is enhanced by the invitation. The Annual Friends Booksale netted almost $15,000 this fall, and again, the public relations benefit of this is outstanding. It is not the purpose here to dwell on friends of libraries projects, but I mention these two as examples of legislative and financial support which a friends group can provide.

In preparation for this paper I interviewed, in person and by telephone, a number of people who work with statewide friends and/or citizens groups. My aim in selecting interviewees was to be representative rather than inclusive. The main reason for this approach is experience with questionnaires. For example, in compiling *A Directory of Friends of Libraries Groups in the United States,*[3] it was almost impossible to be certain that every local and state organization was represented, and we discovered almost immediately after publication that many were missing. Similarly, responses to a national survey conducted by the Colorado state friends group during December 1978 indicated that while those who replied were most helpful, there were unanswered questionnaires. All of us who have conducted research projects using mailed questionnaires have experienced this problem.

Therefore, I approached the subject of "networks of friends" by starting at the national level. The White House conference office supplied some leads, my contacts on the National Friends Committee provided others, and each of these people suggested others. Those to whom I spoke who are involved with statewide friends and citizens groups were helpful, cooperative, and enthusiastic.[4]

Definition and Purpose

At the outset, a definition is needed. "Friends of the library" are those people who believe that any community is a better place in which to live if it has a first-rate library. They have a common concern for their library's active expansion and participation in community life, and they are convinced that good library service is important to everyone.

Local and statewide groups have similar purposes. The following list is a composite of goals and objectives statements from several friends groups:

1. to create and stimulate public support of the library's programs;
2. to interpret the library to the community;
3. to encourage gifts, endowments, and memorials for the library;
4. to provide financial support beyond the library's budget capacity;
5. to work for library legislation and/or appropriations at local, state and national levels;

6. to enlist increased support for libraries from decision-makers;
7. to create and/or intensify community awareness of the library's programs and possibilities;
8. to gain support for library expansion;
9. to campaign for better building facilities;
10. to sponsor programs designed to add to the cultural life of the community;
11. to participate in public relations activities in the community;
12. to provide volunteers for tasks the library cannot support from its budget;
13. to call public attention to outstanding achievements of the staff; and
14. to create understanding of the role of libraries in providing opportunities for education, literacy, and lifelong learning.

Local Organizations

How are friends groups organized and governed? The bylaws and constitutions of seven local friends groups from around the United States were analyzed and compared, and a number of items were found to be common to all. For example, all have a name, a purpose, a membership, officers, duties of officers, an executive board, meetings, dues, funds, and so forth. Several of the bylaws list the address of the association. A few of them, in their statement of "purpose," mention their connection with the library administration and the trustees group. One of the bylaws specifies that the group is not working on behalf of a political candidate. In some instances there is a paragraph telling when the group was originally organized, and several documents indicate under "membership" the types of members and the dues for each category. Most friends organizations have a board of directors in addition to the officers. The size of the boards vary, and in some instances there are detailed descriptions of committee rules and authority.

Statewide Organizations

An example of a statewide friends organization, now in its sixteenth year, is the Friends of Wisconsin Libraries, Inc. (FOWL). The brochure describing its activities states that "[FOWL is] a state wide volunteer organization of Wisconsin citizens interested in supporting, expanding, and improving libraries and library services throughout the state."[5] Four purposes are listed:

1. Our purpose is to be the communicating link between libraries, their communities, and the state; to help inform citizens about

library matters; to be an instrument for potential action in public library affairs; and to seek closer understanding and cooperation between citizens, Trustees, Librarians, and their state organizations.

2. We encourage the formation of new Friends groups, providing
   information and speakers upon request, and inviting interested
   persons to attend our semi-annual workshops.
3. We stimulate existing Friends groups to wider and deeper activity through offering an award each year to the local group
   which has made the most significant contributions to its library's
   program.
4. We work to enlist support from civic leaders and governing
   officials for increased understanding and expansion of modern
   library systems and services.[6]

The brochure further states:

The Board, in addition to the usual officers, consists of the past
president, a member-at-large, and a Director and Assistant from
each of the Wisconsin Congressional Districts. The Board meets
two or three times a year.

The full membership is invited to participate in the fall convention of [the] Wisconsin Library Association, at which FOWL conducts a workshop and sponsors a joint luncheon with the Wisconsin
Trustees Association. . . .

The annual meeting of FOWL is held each spring immediately
after National Library Week in a place selected because of special
library activity in the past year. New buildings, new services to
the community, a new director, or special exhibitions have occa-
sioned the invitation from the local friends group for FOWL to
hold its meeting in their community.

This group has a resource kit containing more than fifty items on such
subjects as how to begin a friends of the library group, how to build membership, and how to plan purposeful service. The kit is available for $5.00,
or $6.50 by mail.[7] There is a quarterly newsletter, as well as occasional let-
ters from the president. In one recent president's letter, Virginia Heinemann
writes:

Due to the distances between members of the executive board a
lot of work is done by committee. Friend of Friends chairman
helps new or established groups with problems and handles the
Library of the Year contest; legislative committee, through the

newsletter or at meetings, keeps the members informed as to pending library-related legislation. . . . I feel that a state Friends organization should be formed through the efforts of local groups. This is where the officers and the directors are taken from. We receive no assistance from the State Library Division, unless we request it. There is a liaison person that attends our general meetings who keeps us informed as to the state problems. Keeping Friends a total citizen-involvement program has kept its growth healthy. With the budget cutbacks imminent in today's tax revolt I predict more and more Friends groups springing up to bridge the gap in services and quality. A state Friends group is a natural outgrowth of this trend.[8]

Samples of FOWL's bylaws, newsletter, and brochures are available upon request.[9]

The Friends of California Libraries also has an information kit in booklet format which discusses forming a friends group, budgeting, program possibilities, publicity, and bond issues for library buildings. This kit is available for five dollars.[10] In response to my request for information about the Friends of California Libraries, James Buckley, director of the Marin County Public Library, wrote:

There appear to be no drawbacks to this state organization of Friends. It has been a positive factor in stimulating the creation of Friends groups and encouraging the growth and activities of established groups. The Friends of California Libraries Newsletter, *Folio,* announces and describes Friends activities and library happenings throughout the state. Both board and advisory board members are available and have spoken to individuals and groups resulting in creation of new Friends groups. In addition, participation by librarians in this organization has resulted in better understanding and cooperation between libraries and their users.[11]

Wisconsin and California have had statewide friends groups for many years. In contrast, citizens in Pennsylvania and Florida have only recently formed statewide groups, as a result of their states' Governor's Conferences on Library and Information Services.

The Pennsylvania Citizens for Better Libraries (PCBL) was created and incorporated on October 20, 1978. One of the resolutions from the Pennsylvania Governor's Conference called for the creation of a statewide organization of friends and advocates of libraries. The thirty delegates picked to represent Pennsylvania at the White House conference served as the planning committee for the new group. Their first annual meeting was held October 17, 1979, using the theme "Lobbying for Libraries: Citizens Make a Difference." PCBL, through its Committee on Legislation, has already developed a structure for a legislative network composed of local friends groups.

The PCBL membership brochure states that "together we can make the public aware of the needs and services of libraries; focus our support for libraries of all types; have a statewide impact on the future of information services; serve as a sounding board for citizen action; influence legislation."[12] The brochure suggests several benefits of membership: "a newsletter with legislative updates; regional workshops on issues and concerns of library advocates; advisory services on organizations, public relations and lobbying; an idea exchange on programs and fund raising; a clearing house for information."[13] The *PCBL Newsletter*[14] is most informative, and minutes of board meetings which were submitted to me as background resource material indicate that a vital and concerned group of professional and lay people are keeping themselves aware of statewide library problems and concerns.

On August 14, 1979, the Council for Florida Libraries was incorporated. Council membership is open to all, and: "recruitment is urged of 'persons and organizations who have achieved a high degree of success and public recognition in the fields of business, industry, commerce, government, education, the arts or the professions. There shall be no political qualifications for membership.' "[15] As set forth in their newsletter:

> This citizens' group, an outgrowth of the Florida Governor's Conference..., is charged with creating greater public awareness of the role of libraries as an important resource for the cultural, educational and economic growth of Florida.
>
> Citizen and library delegates and alternates to the Governor's Conference set the highest priority on enhancing public understanding of "the essential roles of all types of libraries and library services in the economic, cultural, and social life of the community."[16]

The newly created council has been selected by the American Advertising Federation's State of Florida Chapter as its public service project for the coming year. The federation's project coordinator plans "to establish an all-media campaign to build library understanding throughout the state."[17] One of the first programs of the Council for Florida Libraries is a Florida Book and Author Festival scheduled for February 18-29, 1980. In cities throughout the state, talks by authors will be given; each event will be co-sponsored by a local library friends group and the council.

A National Organization

A significant event in friends' support of libraries occurred in June 1979 with the formation of a national organization called Friends of Libraries U.S.A. Minutes from the June 25, 1979, meeting of the National Friends of Libraries Committee reflect that representatives of local friends groups from thirty-four states met with the committee during the American Library Association convention in Dallas. Ruth Frame, Deputy Executive Director of ALA, pledged support for the proposed national organization. Among the issues discussed were:

1. the organizational relationship among ALA, the Library Administration and Management Association, and Friends of Libraries U.S.A.;
2. the relationship between membership in Friends of Libraries U.S.A. and membership in ALA;
3. the role of Friends of Libraries U.S.A. in lobbying activity, particularly in connection with Section 501(c) (3) of the IRS Code;
4. the purposes of the organization as stated in the draft constitution; and
5. the use of the *Friends of the Library National Notebook* as the primary communication vehicle of the organization.

Following the discussion it was unanimously voted that a national organization called Friends of Libraries U.S.A. be formed. The purpose of the national organization is to encourage and assist in the development of friends of libraries groups nationally, to promote the development of excellent library service for all residents of the United States, to provide means for friends of libraries groups to have access to information and ideas that will prove useful in the operation of their organization, and to make the public aware of the existence of friends of libraries groups and the services they perform.

Historical Perspective

We have been looking at local, state and national friends of libraries groups, particularly with regard to recent events; however, there have been friends groups supporting local libraries for more than fifty years. According to the American Library Association, the first groups in the United States to be called "Friends of the Library" began in 1922 in Glen Ellyn, Illinois, and in Syracuse, New York. Both of these groups still exist today.

Friends of public libraries were especially important in the 1930s during the depression. In many places, the initiative for continuing public library services began with citizens who organized into citizens clubs and associations.

Local friends groups usually adapt their goals to meet the needs of their own communities; therefore, their purposes, organizational structures, and contributions are varied. But, as mentioned earlier, there is a core list of activities common to all. There are also friends groups which support academic libraries, special libraries, and school media centers as well as public libraries.[18]

A survey of friends of libraries groups in sixty-four academic, public and special libraries was conducted in 1974, and results of the study were reported in the July 1975 issue of *College & Research Libraries*. This article is recommended because it contains a thorough examination of the origin, objectives, and government of friends groups, as well as an analysis of the structure of membership, activities, types of publications, and problems encountered in the friends groups studied.[19]

Statewide friends groups date to the 1960s, but have increased in number during the past year largely as a result of the governors' conferences. Charles Benton, chairman of the National Commission on Libraries and Information Science, addressed the organizational meeting of Friends of Libraries U.S.A. and cited the excitement in the development of statewide citizens' action groups taking place across the country in support of libraries. He stated that if this were the only outcome of the governors' conferences, the statewide conclaves would be considered successful because they aroused citizens to action.

Networks of Friends

With the organization of local, state, and, now, national friends groups involving all types of libraries, there should be consideration of the idea of networks of friends. How can these groups work together for the good of all libraries? How can they communicate with each other? Will they? What are the advantages and problems of having a network of friends of libraries groups? Is such a network feasible?

In order to consider some of these questions, we must first agree on a definition of "network." Like the term *system,* the word *network* means different things to different people. For present purposes, a network includes a number of libraries or friends groups interconnected by communication links or channels which can be used for the cooperative exchange or transfer of materials and information.[20] A network:

1. implies a formal organization of individual units;
2. provides a way for individual units to work together and to share resources and personnel;
3. expands and/or extends services to an ever-widening area of people;
4. has defined administrative responsibilities;
5. has defined goals and objectives;
6. provides a mechanism for keeping records;

7. enables units to share the costs of developing and producing materials too costly for one unit to bear by itself; and
8. facilitates the standardization of procedures.

Duggan states that: "networks, and the inter-library cooperation they require, offer an opportunity to combine materials, services, and expertise in order to achieve more than any one library can do alone. In this case, the whole is greater than the sum of its parts, for each library can offer its particular patron group the total capability of the network, including outside resources not previously available."[21]

Olson, Shank and Olsen compiled a short list of the essential characteristics of a library and information network:

1. A network's function is to marshal resources from its environment to accomplish results beyond the ability of any one of its members.
2. A network has developed an organizational design and structure that allows it to establish an identifiable domain and exercise appropriate influence over the members.
3. It has a base in communications technology.[22]

Statewide friends and citizens groups have many of these characteristics implicit in their purpose statements.

Networks: Purpose, Organization and Activities

In order for us to consider a network of friends, it is helpful to look at the purpose, organization and activities of networks, and to compare these characteristics with the purpose, organization and activities of friends groups. Let us first consider five rather basic purposes of networks:

1. to share resources in order to accomplish results beyond the ability of any one member;
2. to provide a formal organization for the purpose of sharing resources and personnel;
3. to expand and/or extend services to an ever-increasing number of people;
4. to facilitate standardization of records and procedures and to share ways of more effectively serving constituencies; and
5. to share costs of developing and producing materials and/or technologies too costly for one unit to bear alone.

We are all aware of the spiraling costs of resources in libraries, such as journal subscriptions, books, media, terminals, equipment, and the necessary personnel to serve library users. Every library cannot possibly have everything its patrons request. Therefore, systems and networks provide a means by which even the smallest library may have access to holdings of a larger library through planned programs of sharing. This principle of sharing materials and ideas is applicable to friends groups. Even the smallest friends group can share ideas and materials with larger groups through a network organized for such a purpose. The California and Wisconsin state groups are performing activities of this type.

A network requires commitment, operational management and common purpose. Through formal organization it is possible to carry out legal and fiscal responsibility, planning and contractual commitments in order to serve expanded constituencies better. A review of dozens of purpose statements of friends groups reveals areas of commonality. The following list is representative rather than exhaustive, but it provides a framework which indicates that a network of friends groups, sharing a common purpose, could be of mutual benefit to all:

1. to promote development of excellent library service,
2. to create and stimulate public support for libraries,
3. to create understanding of the role of libraries,
4. to enlist increased support for libraries from decision-makers,
5. to influence government to provide library and information services needed by citizens in a democracy, and
6. to participate in public relations activities on behalf of libraries.

Closely related to the purpose of an association are its activities. Among the more frequently cited services or activities of a network are:

1. to identify patron groups;
2. to identify types and levels of service to meet patron needs;
3. to develop and share resources generously, systematically, and expeditiously;
4. to serve as a public information office;
5. to provide training programs for network personnel and users; and
6. to evaluate services.

By combining their efforts, members of a network may reach increasingly larger and different patron groups. In a mobile and diverse society there is a need for people to have equal access to knowledge regardless of their geographic location. An important network activity is the identification of patron groups and provision for adequate service to all the people in the network area. Public information programs are essential, and a network makes it cost-effective to develop professionally a campaign which tells citizens about the information available to them.

A friends group is formed to serve its own library and community; its activities will, by definition, be local in scope. However, all groups could benefit from shared program ideas, speakers, and practical information on such friends activities as fund raising (book sales, publications, trips, programs); service (volunteers take books to home-bound); information (legislative lunches, tours of library); publications (newsletters, annual reports); grants (special projects, rare books, films); and entertainment (film festivals, parties).

The final comparison has to do with organization. Networks and friends groups show similarities in this area. A network includes: (1) an organizational structure (voluntary or legislated; cooperative consortium); (2) a policy board (elected or appointed; sets goals, objectives, policies); (3) an operational office (paid staff; carries out policies and evaluates services); and (4) communication links or channels (to/from users; interface with other networks; exchange of materials and information). Friends groups, in contrast, are organized so as to contain: (1) a constitution and bylaws for each local unit; (2) a policy board and officers (to set and carry out goals, objectives, programs); (3) membership requirements (dues structure); and (4) communication with members, staff, administration, and other community groups via newsletters, meeting and press releases.

The organization, purpose, and activities of networks indicate that there are advantages to working cooperatively: the whole may accomplish more than its parts. However, as Becker and Pulsifer state: "More than lip-service cooperation is required of members of a network. Formal organization assumes participants recognize the value of membership and are willing to accept certain responsibilities. Participants should share a sense of common purpose and be willing to undertake legal, fiscal, and other contractual commitments to ensure the functional integrity of the network."[23] A network of friends must consider these responsibilities.

Networks of Friends of Libraries

The national group, Friends of Libraries U.S.A., shares a common purpose with statewide groups: to encourage the development of local friends groups. These larger networks produce and provide sample materials about what friends are and how they can be used and have developed how-to-do-it kits to help people who wish to form a friends group. They will also send a representative to talk to a group of interested citizens about forming a friends group.

A regional, state, or national network of friends could be used to encourage the exchange of program ideas and speakers, and to discuss library and community interests. When a friends group has developed a successful program or accomplished an outstanding fund-raising event, this could be shared with other friends groups. Just as many school and transportation districts are developing regional programs, so, too, could friends groups. This in no way destroys local autonomy or independence, but rather it expands and enhances a local group's base for ideas.

Many local and state friends groups have developed legislative networks. Keith Doms, director of the Free Library of Philadelphia and chairman of the Committee on Legislation of the Pennsylvania Citizens for Better Libraries, states that "the network of local friend's groups has the potential to play a strong, affirmative role in moving forward library legislation at both state and federal levels."[24]

There are thousands of interested and concerned citizens around the country who could be linked into a very powerful support group. Lay people do not represent a "vested interest" when they speak on behalf of libraries to their state and national legislators, local committee men and women, mayors, and commissioners. In a talk given at the Joint Mountain, Plains, and Colorado Library Association Convention on October 29, 1979, James Marvin, director of the Topeka (Kansas) Public Library said, "A statewide group of friends could be awesome, when welded together in the common cause of libraries, for their impact on the statewide or national scene." He went on to say: "I feel added strength, indeed, when the head of our library board accompanies me to the capitol for a hearing before our legislative delegation from our county. Later, when bombardment is needed, how good to have the friends understand our problems, be involved in them, and writing and calling on our behalf. Friends groups are a part of the arsenal of library weaponry for effective library service delivery." The political connections of this support group should not be overlooked. A national legislative network could be built on strong local and state groups.

I will briefly suggest two other activities of a friends network: to disseminate information and to be a channel for coordination and communication. Both will require careful planning — but all network operations require planning. Thought must also be given to the idea of having a paid staff person act as a coordinator at the state level — and perhaps at the regional and national levels.

Jeanne Raudenbush, president of the Board of Friends of the Denver Public Library, recently spoke of the idea of having paid coordinators. She commented that if a friends group in a small city (City X) wanted to know how to do a book sale, they could call a state coordinator who would know that City Y, which is approximately the same size, had just completed a successful sale and had written up a detailed plan. On a national scale, it could mean that someone from a very large metropolitan area library could find out about the activities of another metropolitan area friends group without having to depend on the library's professional staff and administration — and their national contacts. She went on to say, "There is a drastic need for more coordination of support groups, and for these groups to unite their efforts, and I feel that this must be done with paid people."[25]

The constitution and bylaws of the Friends of Libraries U.S.A. makes no provision for such a staff position. I feel that this must be addressed in the very near future, as part of the commitment to a functioning national network of friends.

Communication — whatever that means to each of us — is a critical aspect of network activity. A positive contribution to this area is the *Friends of the Library National Notebook* which provides a vehicle for sharing activity ideas and discussing issues.

The governors' pre-White House conferences gave impetus to the need for citizens to be informed and organized in support of libraries. The Florida Governor's Conference on Library and Information Services listed the following resolution as their number one priority:

> Whereas, there is a lack of public awareness at all levels regarding which library services are available; and
>
> Whereas, Florida's citizens need libraries of all types to assist them in everyday living;
>
> Now, therefore, be it resolved that a public and professional awareness program be developed on a local, state, and national level to communicate the essential roles of all types of libraries and library services in the economic, educational, cultural, and social life of the community.[26]

This resolution and many others like it will be presented and considered at the White House Conference on Library and Information Services. As this state-of-the-art paper indicates, the interest, concern and impetus exist for establishing a national network of friends, which would link the local, state, regional, and national groups into what Marvin envisions as an "awesome" library support group. Network development will not occur overnight. It requires management, tact and careful planning, and there will be problems; but I feel that we are well on the way. A national committee of ALA exists; a national organization has been established; and there are state and local groups. The *Notebook* provides one vehicle for communication. A structure for effectively linking these autonomous units is a logical next step.

NOTES

1. Veseley, Marilyn L. "Concerned Delegates" (letter), *Library Journal* 104: 2142, Oct. 15, 1979.

2. Dolnick, Sandy. "Citizens/Friends Together," *Friends of the Library National Notebook* 1:1, Winter 1978.

3. Dolnick, Sandy, comp. *Friends of the Library National Notebook: A Directory of Friends of Libraries Groups in the United States.* Chicago, ALA, Library Administration and Management Association, 1978.

4. I would like to acknowledge that materials and ideas came to me from Barbara Cooper, Secretary of the Council for Florida Libraries; Susan Whittle of the Florida State Library; Lois Albrecht of the State Library of Pennsylvania; Sally Drew of the Wisconsin State Library; and Virginia Heinemann and Denise Wenger, both of the Friends of Wisconsin Libraries, Inc. James and Meg Buckley of the Friends of California Libraries, Nathan Gross of the Citizens for Washington Libraries, Evelyn Brewster of the Colorado State Library, and Jeanne Raudenbush of the Denver Public Library Friends also gave freely of their time and provided me with ideas.

5. Friends of Wisconsin Libraries, Inc. "Introducing Friends of Wisconsin Libraries." FOWL, n.d. (brochure)

6. Ibid.

7. Address inquiries to Friends of Wisconsin Libraries, c/o Mrs. Denise A. Wenger, W244 N. 4840 Hwy. J, Pewaukee, Wis. 53072.

8. Letter from Virginia S. Heinemann, Friends of Wisconsin Libraries, n.d., p. 2. (photocopy)

9. For further information, contact Mrs. Harry Heinemann, Jr., 911 McIndoe St., Wausau, Wis. 54401.

10. Address inquiries to Friends of California Libraries, P.O. Box 4701, Whittier, Calif. 90607.

11. Buckley to Mathews, Oct. 10, 1979.

12. "Pennsylvania Citizens for Better Libraries," PCBL, n.d. (brochure)

13. Ibid.

14. *PCBL Newsletter.* Robert N. Case, ed. Pennsylvania Citizens for Better Libraries, P.O. Box 637, Harrisburg, Pa. 17108.

15. "Council Incorporated at Clearwater Meeting," *Council for Florida Libraries Newsletter* 1:2, Sept. 1979.

16. Ibid., p. 1.

17. Ibid.

18. *See, for example,* Sly, Janice R., and Childer, Louise, eds. *Friends of Florida's Public Libraries.* Tallahassee, State Library of Florida, 1978.

19. Gwyn, Ann, et al. "Friends of the Library," *College & Research Libraries* 36:272-82, July 1975.

20. Corbin, John. "Principles of Networks" (paper presented at the Colorado Interlibrary Loan Workshop). Ft. Collins, Colo., April 25, 1974, p. 2.

21. Duggan, Maryann. "Library Network Analysis and Planning (Lib-NAT)," *Journal of Library Automation* 2:157, Sept. 1969.

22. Olson, Edwin E., et al. "Library and Information Networks." *In* Carlos A.

Cuadra, ed. *Annual Review of Information Science and Technology.* Washington, D.C., ASIS, 1972, vol. 7, p. 279.

23. Becker, Joseph, and Pulsifer, Josephine S. *Application of Computer Technology to Library Processes: A Syllabus.* Metuchen, N.J., Scarecrow Press, 1973, p. 140.

24. Doms, Keith. Quoted *in* "PCBL Plans Legislative Networks," *PCBL Newsletter,* Aug. 1979.

25. Raudenbush to Mathews, telephone interview, Oct. 25, 1979.

26. "Approved Resolutions of Governor's Conference," *Florida Libraries* 29:19, Jan.-Feb. 1979.

ELAINE SEATON

"With Friends Like These . . ."

Friends of the Library: so benign, so helpful, so . . . friendly! Yet, so often
when one mentions the subject to library administrators reactions are heard
which range from, "Oh yes, we had a group years ago, when we had our
new building campaign, but after that they became inactive and quietly
disappeared," or, "Oh, you have a friends group? I keep thinking I should
try to get a group going for my library, but what do you do with them?" to
"Friends? You mean pests! There are days I'd trade them for identifiable
enemies!" Are friends worth the bother? Is it heresy to ask?

This small anthology of case studies has been assembled on the basis
of discussions with many people, in different parts of the country and from
libraries of various sizes. An entire book could be written about the inter-
actions between library administration, the trustees of the library, and the
friends group. There appears to be an endless array of stories, experiences,
and strong feelings among participants in these mini-dramas. The stories
may be individual and different, but some underlying themes emerge when
considering the whole:

1. When there is a major purpose or issue, friends can be inspired and
   mobilized to work hard and effectively.
2. Many friends groups seem to be born of a crisis, such as a bond issue
   campaign or a censorship challenge. Let us, for the moment, assume they
   achieve honor and success. During a period of specific need, most friends
   organizations function well.
3. When there is no longer a major issue to channel the drive and energy
   of friends, resolute efforts are required to maintain vitality and interest
   on the part of friends.
4. The "care and feeding" of friends is a constant task, which requires considerable "overhead" in staff time and involvement.
5. Staff members are thus prone to feel the threat of volunteers taking over,
   or to resent what they perceive as extra work.
6. Meanwhile, the friends group itself needs to be encouraged to develop
   "new blood" and avoid the "in-group" syndrome.
7. Power struggles are not uncommon between friends and administrators

and/or trustees. The personality of the leaders of these respective groups is crucial.

8. Clear communication and active liaison are imperatives for success.

By way of illustrating these points, let me share some of the cases I learned about, and point to some of the patterns they reveal.

The Community Celebrity

Some years ago, in one of our country's urban centers, a prominent author was enticed to become president of the local friends of the library group. At first, everyone was thrilled that such a celebrity would be willing to take on the role. What publicity for the library! What prestige! People joined the group, in part, to meet and be associated with this renowned personality.

The key word indeed was "personality." As time wore on, it became ever clearer that people were dealing with an egocentric and eccentric person. The individual was virtually incompetent at organization work. There was no working with others, no planning, no communication. Under the helm of this nonleader, the friends started to deteriorate. Records were not kept. When membership renewals came in, they were not acknowledged. New members would join and then not hear a word. There were no meetings. This prominent person would come once a year to a library board meeting and deliver a report. For five years, the identical report was made — a mouthing of platitudes about plans for the coming year. And no one challenged the situation. Though recognized as unreasonable, the person was "local big celebrity" — a sticky situation indeed.

Gradually, the director of the library began openly to discourage people from joining the friends. Through a series of behind-the-scenes maneuvers, it was finally agreed that a kind of coup d'état was the only way out. Planned and arranged in advance, and following careful parliamentary procedures ("machinations" was the word used to describe this), a special membership meeting of friends was called for the purpose of electing a new slate of officers for the group. The troublesome "personality kid" was advised about what was coming, and given the chance to save face by "arranging" to be needed elsewhere on the appointed day. As can be imagined, the ousted president became a bitter enemy of the library.

Fortunately, the impact of that person's ire was mitigated somewhat. Many people had become aware of the situation and had come to recognize the incompetence plus irrational and irascible qualities of that individual. The revived friends group began to function and to contribute to the library soon thereafter. As constituted today, the organization now has as president a person who concurrently serves as a trustee on the library board and was previously a working city librarian. I am further assured by the head librarian that this arrangement is working beautifully. There must be a lesson to the story; one wonders how many groups have been themselves trapped by the lure of the "community celebrity."

Some Friends Are Like Morris the Cat

Here follows the tale of a library and the several lives of its friends group. Life 1 was that of the kitten. In one of the many suburban communities that sprang up after World War II, a group of people had banded together to create a library where none had previously existed. The group had a very strong leader, and these friends worked enthusiastically and energetically for about four years to bring a library into existence. There were fund-raising parties and events to arouse community awareness. The library began its life in a converted store. The friends contributed hundreds of hours of labor. They painted walls and sanded shelves. They typed borrowers' cards from preregistration forms, alphabetized catalog cards, unpacked books and shelved them. In those early days, they were a cohesive group and had a common, realizable goal. For a period of years after the library began to operate, the group became quiescent and caught its breath — perchance a catnap.

Life 2, then, was that of the pussycat. Next came the drive to buy land and build a "real library." Once again, the friends went to work. They prepared mailings, held house-to-house gatherings to discuss the proposed referendum, conducted a telephone campaign, and got out the vote. Perhaps the surging enthusiasm of "round (life) one" was lacking, but they worked hard and did a fine job. And when the new building was a reality — functioning, beautiful, providing almost undreamed-of services — what then? The friends had nothing to do.

The cataclysm inevitably followed. The group began to look for things to do. They began to poke around, they bothered the staff and were on the way to becoming a considerable nuisance. Neither the trustees nor the director had any real idea of what to do with the group. (In truth, they probably wanted it to go quietly away.) Floundering for a goal, the friends started a newsletter. Since it was "their" newsletter, no one from the library paid too much attention until a fiasco ensued. One of the friends came up with an idea to arrange a charter tour to a foreign country. When people signed up for the trip their "ticket" was put in a raffle. The prize was a free trip. All good intentions and innocence notwithstanding, many in the community were incensed. The tour was regarded as a commercial venture benefiting a particular travel agent. Furthermore, it had no relevance to the library. All disclaimers that it was the friends' idea, not planned or endorsed by the library, were futile in affecting the public's attitude.

The friends and the library are inevitably perceived as *the library*. Anything and everything done by friends reflects on the library. Administrators and trustees who fail to find the time to invest their energies in constantly working with and guiding their friends will incur considerable peril. They are almost certainly courting the "if anything can go wrong, it will" syndrome.

There is a final fillip to the story of the group just described. Some time later, the trustees of the library decided to enlist the help of a consultant in order to reactivate and redirect the friends. After a close look at the situation, the consultant concluded that the library was in a stage of development which did not need the active workings of friends; that, in fact, continuation of the group was counterproductive, a drain on staff time and energy more urgently needed to concentrate on many new services and procedures which the new building had made possible. The consultant advised the board on a "no go" course, recommended that the group be dissolved, and helped effect a graceful exit. The friends had $4000 in their treasury. They made a last great gesture and donated the money for the purchase of a grand piano, a valuable acquisition entirely appropriate to the high level of cultural programs which the library was sponsoring.

Understanding the Friends' Role

Another story highlights a pitfall, as it also raises a secondary point for consideration. One community found its friends group disaffected with some of the library's trustees. When a vacancy developed, the friends put up a candidate. Independent of the friends, another citizen decided to run for the same seat. The friends organization had a very high membership roster. With dues of only one dollar there were more than 1000 members. In point of fact, there were only about twenty people active in the group. But many people in the community drew the conclusion: if the friends of the library were backing one candidate, he must be "the good guy," while the other candidate was "the enemy." Not only were the facts misleading, but the other candidate was elected. It was thus presumed that this trustee would be unwelcome, not being "the library's choice." The new trustee thus took up board responsibilities under unnecessarily inauspicious circumstances.

A clearer understanding of their role would have enabled these friends to act quite differently. Friends can encourage good people to run for the board without waging a campaign for a chosen candidate. They can encourage a board to consider new areas of service, new directions, without becoming surrogate trustees. They can focus attention on problems and generate community support for improved library service. But friends are *not* the policy-makers for the library. Great care should be taken to avoid creating a situation in which anyone who does not belong to their organiza-tion or share their viewpoint is thus not on "the side of the angels."

This story spotlights a secondary debatable point. It is not unusual to find in many organizations dues-paying members in numbers far exceeding a small contingent of active workers. This case makes one wonder whether a friends group is better off aiming for perhaps a smaller membership, but a membership consciously involved, informed about, and committed to the library. Dues should be kept low so that everyone who is interested can join. Friends groups should be inclusive organizations, not exclusive. A person may find it easier to contribute a dollar to a good cause than to experience the bother or embarrassment of saying no; but true and reliable friends are characterized by other attributes.

Library Friends and the Community

Another complex and interesting story involves a friends group which came to the librarian's side in an issue involving censorship. However praise-worthy, that action seriously contributed to exacerbating an existing though yet unidentified problem. For most of its history, the community had been fairly rural in character, populated by a wealthy, highly conservative elite. But over the years, imperceptibly, the community had been changing. It had expanded in numbers, as well as in its socioeconomic makeup. Many newer residents were of the middle and lower-middle classes. A nearby city had begun to encroach. At about that juncture, members of the older, estab-lished part of the community raised a hue and cry and began to demand the removal of some magazines from the library's collection, objecting to the content of titles like *Playboy*. And lo and behold, the newer citizens in the communtiy were siding with the old-timers! The friends leaped into the fray to champion the library's cause. This, bewilderingly, consolidated the opposition. The friends found themselves criticizing the newcomers. No doubt inadvertently, the friends had wrapped themselves in the holier-than-thou banner of "we're the friends, we're on the side of good and right," and, while perhaps not blatantly, the opposition became "the bad guys."

No one could understand why the newcomers were siding with the arch-conservative old-timers. Didn't these (new) people know that the friends were their (more liberal) natural friends/allies? Sentiment in the community heated up.

It took some time for the real issue to surface. The library had not ade-quately recognized and responded to the information needs of the newer residents. Here were people who had practical problems. "Why is the library spending my hard-earned money on 'garbage' when they don't have any good books on how to upholster a couch, repair my car, etc? I'm a taxpayer here, too, and I'm not going to vote for a budget so that they can buy more dirty books." By the time these underlying feelings and attitudes began to be understood, the library and the friends were in deep trouble. The administrator sought help from an outside consultant, who managed to unravel and interpret the situation. Thus, the friends were enabled to shift their emphasis and tone. They stopped attacking, they stopped "labeling" opponents. A new positive stand was taken, quietly, simply favoring the rights of all to have their information needs served by the library, endorsing access to information.

What started as a positive instance of friends defending the library against a censorship attack, altered to their (the friends) becoming part of the problem. Here was a situation in which no one — not the librarian, not the trustees, or the friends — had understood the real issue. It had practically nothing to do with understanding their respective roles. But once the friends were embroiled, they were once again *the library*.

There are times when the services of an outsider can be usefully employed. Serving as a catalyst, such a person can facilitate a group's movement away from an untenable position, and still remain sensitive to the ego involvement of friends the library wants to remain friends.

Positive Encounters

But let us also recall some cheerful tales. In Dallas a friends group, nurtured by careful liaison, took on the major task of helping the library acquire a new building site. Over a period of about fifteen years, the friends have been supportive and have taken the lead in bond issue campaigns. The group has served as a conduit for major and minor gifts for the new building. While providing continuing support for the library's rare book collection, plus an annual appropriation for continuing education scholarships, the friends respond to specific requests for help from the administration — to the extent that their treasury can provide. One staff member describes the group as "born of crisis," working for a specific goal, and directed and encouraged by consistent contact from a single staff member assigned as liaison. This echoes nicely one response received for the recent friends survey. When asked about the areas of library activity of special interest to friends, the reply was an emphatic request to libraries to: "[*tell us the*] specific area of responsibility. If you tell us what you need and want, we'll do it."

In a New Jersey suburban community some years ago, the administrator gained the help of a friends group to launch a series of demonstration projects. The friends provided seed money to begin a framed picture collection, to establish a young adult room, plus other ventures. With the new service as a pilot project, in each case the library succeeded in getting the city to allocate funds so that these services became regular budget-supported features. Talking recently to that administrator about what made that friends group so successful, the answer was almost the same as in Dallas — specific goals, and active, continuous liaison.

Effects of Proposition 13

The impact of Proposition 13, meanwhile, has had its effect on libraries in a variety of ways. In some cases the results have been unexpectedly positive, despite the intrinsic difficulties; in others, distressing. Not only have some California libraries faced severe budget cuts, but the Proposition 13 atmosphere has also led to conflict between professionals and their boards of supervisors.

In one community a board rejected the librarian's plan, which called for curtailed service hours in certain branches, after receiving pressure from the affected local residents. It is hardly necessary to cite specific outcomes of this type of conflict to see the damaged interrelationships (governing body/library/community) that might result in some communities.

What began in one county as a setback for local libraries resulting from Proposition 13 cuts, however, actually stimulated an unexpected boon in library services for two communities. Budget cuts closed both of the small branch buildings, which had been operating in leased quarters, were in poor repair, and located in low-income rural areas. The residents were incensed at the prospect of losing their libraries. They were determined to have library service continue. With guidance from the county librarian, and mutual understanding, they set to work as volunteers at the branches. At the same time, they raised funds locally, formulated plans, and filed for a Community Development Bloc Grant. The result was a two-year grant for $150,000 in one community and a one-year grant in the other. A new prefabricated library building has been built in one town, and a remodeled building on a site purchased by the county in the other. It was not easy; the friends had to convince the board of supervisors that the money was going for a worthwhile project. The library found itself enmeshed in a web of legal problems: insurance coverage for volunteers in a public building, temporary leases, as well as such questions as who would pay for utilities. But as a model for working together in the face of adversity, we could all do well to emulate this relationship between the library and its friends.

A rather different situation shows what can happen when friends go off on their own. A county governing group was considering whether to utilize bookmobiles. Friends leaped in and became a support group for the officials in their plan. The libraries found themselves recipients of bookmobiles.

Subsequently, when the friends wanted to bring pressure of a different sort on the governing body, they found themselves compromised by their earlier action. They thought it would be like "yelling at a guest in one's own house." The story highlights the diffused and often confused relationship between the two groups.

All over California friends have served as library volunteers; and even when things went smoothly, friends learned that keeping a library operating was not as simple as it had seemed initially. There is perhaps even a bit of irony that in some instances the friends who had so willingly volunteered subsequently came to exercise their influence as citizens to press officials for restored fiscal support for their libraries. In some communities, a measure of distrust by staff greeted friends volunteers. Through experience librarians have learned that it is crucial to prepare a formal, written, structured program for volunteers. Volunteers, administrators, and staff alike need to know specifics: "Why are volunteers here, what are they supposed to accomplish?" Clarity in planning and objectives is the key to successful involvement and coordination of a volunteer program.

Being a Friend Means Making a Friend

There are also tales of determined do-gooders who did good. In one well-to-do community, for instance, the library had functioned for many years in a totally inadequate building never designed to serve as a library. Trustees had attempted to get a bond issue referendum on the ballot, but could not influence village authorities to schedule it. The friends, having amassed a considerable reserve fund, put it to work to counter the village government's obstructive stance. By a postcard poll they substantiated the library's claim that the community wanted a new building. They paid for the services of a respected library consultant and to have plans drawn up (something the library could not do without village authorization for such an expenditure). Excellent newspaper coverage resulted, and finally the village board felt pressured to schedule a referendum. Despite the tactic of holding the vote on a holiday weekend in the middle of winter, the friends' hard work brought out the library's supporters, and victory was achieved. These efforts had taken years. All through the period, the friends met regularly with the director of the library, and they gave their library support in a way that conformed to its purpose. When success was achieved their generosity was fully acknowledged, their prestige enhanced.

This all happened several years ago, but this friends group continues to provide the library with steady, substantial financing for special programs of outstanding distinction. The library, it should be noted, selects the programs. Decisions are made in conference with a friends committee, but the library retains the ultimate authority. Everyone recognizes that if there are negative repercussions to a particular program, the library suffers directly, the friends only tangentially. And human nature being what it is, some old-timers come to programs at that library today and announce proudly how they voted to make the building possible, with its extra-special meeting room. The staff and friends may know that these persons had actually been opposed; but because being a friend means making a friend for the library, the proper response is to nod pleasantly and say, "Oh yes, isn't it great?"

The Importance of Communication

In matters of scheduling programs, a contrasting unhappy situation in another community shows what happens in the absence of a clear delineation of who sets policy. At issue was the use of the library's meeting room. This was a relatively small library, and the friends took responsibility for arranging programs. Inevitably, the friends planned an event and the director said no. In short order, friends, trustees, and librarian were embroiled in a divisive squabble. Friends assumed the position that if they did the work, they should have the authority. It was by now obvious to everyone that roles had never been defined. Communication was lacking, or at best, irregular. Where once there were friends, there were now angry and abusive citizens. The problem resulted in mayhem between the board and its own director. Everyone lost, no one won.

Are personalities the key? There is the case of one large city library which enjoyed the support of a friends group for several years. The president of the friends was regarded by many as a difficult, opinionated individual. But the administrator and the president of the friends had an easy, comfortable relationship. If they didn't see eye to eye on a question, they would talk about it, think about it, talk about it some more, and work out an agreement.

Then the librarian left the city for a new position and a new director was hired. The smooth working relationship between friends and library was disturbed. No real problem surfaced for a time. Then trouble began to brew. The library administration had made certain priority decisions concerning the location of branches. The friends had their own ideas about where branches should be placed. A conflict of major proportion developed between the friends' leader and the director of the library. So serious was their falling-out that the director had the friend barred from the library. So strong a driving force had the leader been that without that person the friends group disintegrated. The administrator blamed the failure on the the personality of the leader, claiming that he was obsessed with prestige and power. As a note to this story, I've been told that some time ago a major consulting firm was asked to evaluate the factors that contribute to success in the operation of a library system. Several thousand dollars later, the major conclusion was that the single biggest factor affecting success is the personality of the top person in the organization.

In another library, a friends group volunteered to do a community survey in order to find out how people felt about the library being open on Sundays. The director was aware and enthusiastic. The circulation desk clerks, however, had no idea that the director planned to budget for additional staff, and resented the whole scheme. A friend overheard a staff member remarking to a patron: "Tell that woman you don't favor Sunday openings. Think of the extra work for us!" Clearly, in this case there was a communication gap between librarian and staff, as well as friends and staff.

Another well-intentioned friends project — an incentive grant to garner ideas from staff members that would lead to innovative library programs — backfired. The staff reaction was, "one more example of the friends creating extra work, and trying to tell us how to do our jobs!" This particular near-fiasco was rescued by one friend who recognized the resistance and spent a good deal of time chatting individually with various staff members, informally explaining the anticipated advantages of having "seed money" to try out new ideas.

Staff members may perceive volunteers as "wanting to take over the library." In one library a president of the friends group overheard a tirade, one staff member to another, against the friends volunteers. Fortunately, the president and library director viewed this as a joint problem; neither decided "fault," and after quietly investigating the problem it was agreed that the particular project was counterproductive and should be gradually phased out, redirecting friends efforts to other activities.

Conclusion

There are obviously numerous pitfalls on the path that friends and their libraries tread: power struggles, personality clashes, lack of clearly defined roles, time demands on administrator and staff — these are just a few. Administrators must be prepared to commit themselves to friends, truly to want them. Communication must be open and sensitive. When there is no major goal for friends to work on, motivating the group from day to day will demand energy and creative thinking by the librarian.

Why do some friends groups fade away? They may have been organized only for a crisis and do not have, or do not soon thereafter develop, long-range goals. Sometimes the leadership dies off or moves away. Not uncommonly, the most active friends become trustees; the lifeblood of the group is drained. Personal reasons may intervene, such as loss of interest or lack of time. All these reasons and more may be present, and it must always be asked: is this necessarily bad?

Friends ideally function *on behalf of* the library, not *as* the library. But we librarians who want friends to be effective need to see them as an important part of our job. Keeping a friends group active, an asset to the library, requires communication, active liaison, sensitivity, clear guidelines as to roles, and something to do. It takes our best effort as professionals, which really means as people.

One respondent to Sandy Dolnick's survey has aptly expressed the basic "simple rules of friendly behavior: consideration, respect, tolerance, understanding, appreciation, self-sacrifice, patience and tact should characterize the friends' and librarian's relationship." The librarian should be further reminded of the sign which Edward Koch, mayor of New York, is said to have on his desk. It reads, "If you say it can't be done, you're right."

PAUL H. MOSHER

Friends Groups and Academic Libraries

The first university library friends group was founded at Harvard in 1925, in order to provide "the most effective aid" for that library. In all probability, the organization was established to stimulate the flagging enthusiasm of donors, whose benefactions had begun to decline; and it was probably modeled on the first library support organization to call itself a friends group, La Société des Amis de la Bibliothèque Nationale et des Grandes Bibliothèques de France, which had been founded in 1913, and with which Harvard's library director, Archibald Coolidge, had become familiar during a tour and book-buying expedition to Europe.[1]

By 1930 there were emulative friends groups at Columbia, Yale, Princeton, and Johns Hopkins, and the number grew substantially during the next four decades. While the process of growth has been substantial, it has undergone fluctuations; there has been a fairly high mortality rate among friends groups. The number swells during periods of poor library funding or rapidly rising costs, and it declines during times of plenty; for example, there were few new groups between 1954 and 1970,[2] but significant multiplication of them occurred during the decades immediately preceding and following that period. There has also been a tidal ebb and flow as groups have lost direction or membership, or as major projects have been completed. Successive editions of the ALA Friends of the Library Committee publications show that of thirty-five groups listed in 1937, twenty-four were not listed in 1951; and of eighty-eight listed in 1941, fifty-nine groups were not mentioned in 1951, and fifty were missing in 1955.[3] However, groups which became moribund have sometimes been reactivated. Groups are presently active in support of about one-half of the ARL libraries.[4]

The typical academic research library friends group was organized by the library director working in conjunction with alumni and faculty. It has about 600 members and a number of membership categories, with dues ranging from $10 to $500. The group is governed by a president, a vice president, a secretary-treasurer, and a program chairman; an executive committee consisting of those officers acts as a steering committee for a board of fourteen, which governs the organization. The library director serves ex officio on the board.

This typical group raises funds for library purchases, builds the special collections of the library, issues publications, builds community support for the library, and conducts lectures and other library- and book-related social and cultural events. The group raises about $25,000 each year through dues in order to provide for its activities and to support notable library acquisitions, though this support can represent only a portion of the $25,000 raised. The activity of the group is furthered by a library staff member who acts as liaison officer, and the library provides the group with some clerical support and office space.

While the group is generally regarded as useful and beneficial, it does present a few problems for its library; chief among them are policy or authority disputes, work overload of library staff, minimal financial contribution, and membership or fiscal problems and complications.

The following statements of missions and goals summarize clearly the theoretical reasons for the existence of such groups. The Johns Hopkins brochure describes the friends' role as "to assume the responsibility of acquainting its members with the resources and needs of the university library and to create from dues or income a fund for the purchase of those materials most likely to enhance the lasting value of the library."[5] The Rutgers Friends take a more long-term and developmental turn: to "maintain an organization of persons interested in books, to assist in bringing to the library funds for special needs beyond the command of the library budget, to encourage gifts of books and manuscripts, and to cooperate with the librarian and the library advisory board in the development of resources of the library."[6]

Here, I will move briefly from the general to the specific. The Stanford Library Associates, with which I am affiliated, is one of the newer friends groups in major academic research libraries. The organization was established in 1973 by collaboration between an extraordinarily energetic and visionary friend and faculty member, Paul Hanna, and our library director, David Weber, in recognition of the library's need for extraordinary development efforts to help offset materials cost increases — both during budget equilibrium programs of the late 1960s and from recognition that the 1970s and 1980s would probably bring greater constraints. Our friends group assists the library in many ways in dealing with fiscal restraint and its threat to the development and improvement of library research and teaching collections. It also enables the library to acquire extraordinary titles or collections in order to improve the quality of its holdings beyond the capacity of its budget or normal collecting priorities.

The Associates' membership is now nearing 550, having risen 61 percent in the last two years, thanks to hard and productive work by its officers and the library development officer, a splendid program of events, and a high level of support by library staff. The organization of the group is fairly standard; I will concentrate on useful divergences from the pattern. There is a chairman, a vice chairman, a secretary-treasurer, and a membership chairman. The executive committee consists of these officers plus the immediate past chairman and an elected at-large member from the board of directors, which consists of eighteen members and meets quarterly. The executive committee governs between board meetings, but the board ultimately decides everything from major programs and gifts to the color of the napkins at receptions. We have sought to attract as members prominent California book dealers, collectors and printers, as well as prominent and wealthy citizens, and friends and students who love and use books and libraries.

The Stanford Library Associates sponsor an impressive annual series of programs including lectures, tours, picnics, and dramatic or musical presentations, which are coordinated with special collections exhibits and bibliographic or bibliophilic themes. Last summer, they conducted a library tour of Great Britain, which was a great success, and a William Morris tour of England is planned for summer 1980. A library tour of France is in the planning stages.

The organization has an ambitious publications program including membership brochures, keepsakes, and a highly attractive and informative journal, *The Imprint of the Stanford Libraries Associates,* which contains articles on books, collections and libraries around the world, as well as news of the Associates and important Stanford Library programs. Since the group, as well as our special collections staff, includes lovers of fine printing and a number of fine printers, typographical standards are high. The publications, like the program of activities, represent value given and have helped to increase the size and quality of the friends group.

An additional program element of the Stanford Library Associates is building what Robert Vosper calls the supportive or "contrapuntal" relationship between private book collecting and institutional collection building in this country.[7] Vosper, a charter member of the Stanford Library Associates and former Library Visiting Committee member (as well as UCLA University Librarian Emeritus and former ALA president), writes:

> The interweaving of the private with the institutional tone of collection building in modern research libraries is further evident in the flowering of organized community friends of libraries groups such as the Associates of the Stanford University Libraries in the years since 1950. Not only do private collectors form a significant part of the membership of those generous bodies, but the result in most cases, over and beyond direct gifts of books, is the creation of a special purchase fund which can be deployed more in the pri-

vate mode of book buying than in the routine institutional style. Most important, though, a group such as the Associates provides moral support for the library program and it assures a setting that will be encouraging for private benefactors.[8]

One of the most important and productive aspects of the Associates is the work of a full-time library development officer (whose salary funding is shared by the library and the University Office of Development, and which has been recovered many times over in gifts, endowments, and grants) as the group's secretary-treasurer and library liaison; I will return to this matter shortly. The chief of special collections and his staff, the university archivist, and the gifts-and-exchange head are also regular participants in the group's activities, as are a number of our chief bibliographers. The director of libraries and associate director for collection development also work closely with the group in its activities. We have encouraged a level of exchange and mutual education between friends and the library that is high without being stifling.

The Associates have been active in supporting special collections through gifts and funds, have set up endowments for book purchases, and have played an important role in our current National Endowment for the Humanities matching-fund campaign for books in the humanities. We get a maximum of gifts from the group through periodic, carefully orchestrated presentations of "gift lists," which suggest a number of potential gift items with descriptions, outlines of need, faculty letters of support, or presentations with illustrations, such as photocopies of title pages. The Associates have also visited virtually every branch and coordinate library on campus, and have often presented appropriate books or pieces of needed equipment as commemorations of their visits.

A few remarks need to be made on the theory and role of friends groups. These groups must not exist in a vacuum if they are to realize their greatest potential for library support. From the existing literature and from experience, I would suggest that many libraries have tapped only a portion of the development potential of such groups. Each friends organization should be part of a coherent library development program geared to the larger mission and goals of the library within the developmental context of the university as a whole. A friends group is a segment or a unit, certainly a vital one, of a library's *total* long-range development program, and its members, singly or in groups, offer a number of forms of support and aid beyond occasional gifts for special collections.

An academic library's friends group must be the library's alumni organization — the equal of that of any college or school — even though the library has, technically speaking, no alumni. The friends group has the additional advantage of being a *neutral* alumni group because the academic library is essentially a nonpolitical agency in an institution fraught with political antagonisms or disillusionments involving alumni and students or campus administrators. Study of the literature on library friends groups revealed no emphasis on the friends as a library's alumni, but I believe this analogy is significant and useful. Their contributions range well beyond books and funds, community relations efforts, and programs which bring alumni, faculty, librarians, and other friends together. Friends groups can be vital sources of information, contacts, and volunteers who help to solicit prospects and to move forward programs of library development of greater scope and significance than the more immediately programmatic results of friends group efforts as such. As individuals, they can provide gifts of collections, individual titles, funds, and bequests quite apart from their activity as friends or volunteers. A friends group is often only one of a number of developmental organizations within a library or university structure; others include visiting committees, campaign committees, volunteer groups, and annual fund committees, each of which has a rather different role in the larger developmental frame, and each of which draws from the resource pool provided by a friends group. Friends groups allow the opportunity to consider and prepare members for service on these other developmental or counseling groups, and for other university volunteer development activity.

It may reasonably be suggested that library friends groups cost more than they are worth in academic libraries if they exist only for their gifts of books or book funds (totaling, on the average, $7,000–$10,000 per year). Friends groups should be understood in terms of long-term developmental goals, primarily as a recruiting ground for other developmental activities and as a means of attracting personal gifts and bequests.

At Stanford, we try to bring the library's subject or area bibliographers into contact with the Associates. This is done as a deliberate program of mutual benefit in order to bring friends to a closer understanding of the library's relationship to academic programs, and thus closer to the work of teaching and scholarship that is the essence of our institution, and in turn, to make our librarians more consciously active agents in our development program. In addition to participation in the group's events and meetings, the bibliographers receive basic training in library and university development policies and practices from our library development officer. As endowment funds are solicited or received in support of ongoing library acquisition in a specified area — English literature, for example — the appropriate bibliographers maintain contact with donors, describe specific library needs of faculty and students, and report to donors of specific funds on selected purchases made with fund revenues. This program appears unusual in library development activities, but has already proved its worth at Stanford in several concrete situations.

Once a library development program is constructed on a friends base, and a level of continuing activity is reached, results begin to multiply. The process of building up to such a level of ongoing activity is rather like the Japanese game of *Go*, in which moves are made in such a way as to create and multiply the largest number of favorable options and possibilities for future moves. Once a level of productive activity is built up, its continued operation is rather like conducting a symphony orchestra, with the development officer acting as conductor or concertmaster.

I will construct an example to illustrate: friends member A is active and effective, has substantial means, and a wide network of friends and acquaintances. Friend A is then asked to serve on the visiting committee. As the result of productive and active membership on the visiting committee, A is asked, along with friends members B and C and visiting committee member D, to set up a blue-ribbon task force to raise endowment money for NEH matching-grant funds. A, B, C, and D, with the development officer and the collection development officer, choose other task force members, including interested, knowledgeable, and articulate faculty and librarians.

As a result of meetings, the identification of needs, and goals, lists of prospects and volunteers, and a variety of activities and solicitations, $300,000 is raised for endowed humanities book funds, thus bringing in $100,000 in federal matching money. But, as spin-offs of a raised level of activity and awareness, a $250,000 literature collection is given to the library (which brings an additional $80,000 in federal matching money), a task force member pays for a renovated special collections reading room, a friend endows a chair in French, and a whole group of friends, librarians, faculty, and development office staff have an exciting, informative, and productive time working together. I cannot overemphasize the strong sense of community, mutual understanding, and common pursuit of goals that results when such an effort is successfully constructed and executed. It should be noted that throughout such a campaign the committee and the library must work closely with the development office staff. This clarifies priorities, ensures that prospects are not cross-solicited, and can also serve as a program of the library development office, a process quite as important as development work with volunteers or prospects.

This story, or a scaled version of it, could happen to your library. It could *not* have happened without the library friends, without a professional development officer to coordinate planning, staffing, and phasing, or without the willing and enthusiastic participation of volunteers: lay, librarian, and faculty.

Finally, I would like to emphasize that one doesn't make money without investing time and money. Development work in a library is a long-term process carried out over years, decades and generations, and should not be regarded as a short-term, single campaign. The investment in development using library friends as a base is not, however, appropriate only for large, wealthy universities; it can take place in most libraries, scaled and shaped by local goals and available resources. The specific annual contributions of a friends group would often scarcely justify the existence of the group, to say nothing of the investment of library staff effort and office space, but the periodic or annual gifts of such a group should properly be seen as only the tip of the development iceberg; the longer-term investment should be seen as bequests, significant donations of books or endowment, or the action of friends as volunteers in soliciting or approaching other benefactors over a period of years.

It is the role of friends groups as resource and recruiting pools for long-term, ambitious, and multiple campaign efforts that I have wished to underline here. Friends groups should not be seen as ends in themselves for most libraries, but as sources and resources for a range of short- and long-term developmental activities having as their goal the larger financial benefit of the library. Through carefully nurturing those resources, a library can gain better support, better collections and better service for generations of library users yet to come.

NOTES

1. Wallace, Sarah L., ed. *Friends of the Library: Organization and Activities.* Chicago, ALA, 1962, p. 4.

2. Association of Research Libraries. Systems and Procedures Exchange Center. "Friends of the Library Organizations," SPEC Flyer No. 6, April 1974. (News release.) *See also* _____. *SPEC Kit 6: Friends of the Library Organizations.* 1974.

3. Wallace, op. cit., p. 9.

4. Association of Research Libraries, *SPEC Kit 6,* op. cit.

5. Brewer, Frances J. "Friends of the Library and Other Benefactors and Donors," *Library Trends* 9:459, April 1961.

6. Ibid.

7. Vosper, Robert. "The Private Collector and the Research Library: A Goodly Company," *The Imprint of the Stanford Libraries Associates* 4:11, 1978.

8. Ibid., p. 12.

THOMAS G. SANBERG

The Development Function

Development is an appropriate term for describing the essential function which sustains most nonprofit, contribution-reliant institutions. To develop is to activate or to grow; the development function is concerned with promoting growth. Often, in the context of the nonprofit organization, development is considered to be synonymous with fund raising; the function is seen exclusively as one of raising money. Actually, the development function is much more inclusive. Fund raising is the result of development, not the essence.

Librarians working for tax-supported libraries rather than private, nonprofit organizations are understandably interested in ways to develop the funds necessary to compensate for budget cuts and increased costs. The ideas under discussion here apply to both not-for-profit and tax-supported institutions, although the frame of reference will most frequently be nonprofit organizations.

The development function includes a variety of activities which promote growth. First, however, it is important to understand how development fits into an organization's overall structure. In most nonprofit institutions, some group of people, often the membership, elects trustees or a board of directors. The board establishes broad policy and hires a chief executive officer (CEO). The CEO has the day-to-day operating authority and is responsible for effecting the policy established by the board. The CEO may hire an executive vice president and one or more vice presidents to manage the main departments. Frequently these include vice presidents for finance, for development, for programs, and for operations.

More progressive organizations generally allocate operating decisions to the executive vice president and to the vice presidents for programs and operations, while the responsibility for planning is allocated to the vice presidents for development and finance. In other words, involvement with day-to-day operations is not the responsibility of the development department.

This has both positive and negative aspects. The vice president for development may feel excluded from the daily operation of his organization, although it is his efforts which make possible the institution's long-term

77

survival. On the other hand, because he is not burdened with responsibility for operations, the development officer is free to devote himself to long-range planning and to activities which make future growth possible. Furthermore, the development professional may be comforted by the fact that innovation is usually initiated by his branch of the organization. This bifurcation between long-range development planning and day-to-day operations is the key to the successful, efficient functioning of the not-for-profit institution.

It is not possible to attend adequately to the development function *and* to supervise operations. There is an overwhelming amount of work in the development area, and the number and size of projects increase geometrically as the organization achieves increasingly greater success.

The development function basically includes two activities: fund raising, and communications, which is more commonly called "public relations." The development officer is responsible for both. In a very large organization a vice president for development may have both a director of development and a director of public relations reporting to him or her. However, the fund-raising and public relations activities are not always separate and distinct: more often than not, they overlap and sometimes merge. Fund-raising activities include capital campaigns, annual operating funds campaigns, special events, deferred-giving programs, and volunteer development. Public relations responsibilities include publicity, publications, community relations and presentations, and government relations. Generally, both fund-raising and public relations activities require planning, budgeting, administration, and record keeping. Let us examine each of these elements.

First, development is planning. Planning is the initial and continuing process of evaluating an organization's strengths and weaknesses, needs and goals. It is the creation of projects which maximize strengths, overcome weaknesses, fulfill needs, and effect goals.

Well-administered organizations periodically "audit" themselves. The development officer must be a key person in the administrative process by which the internal and external strengths and weaknesses of the institution are thoroughly and objectively assessed. A description of the organizational audit is a seminar topic in itself. Briefly, however, it involves an effort to quantify important factors. Is the service being delivered increasing or decreasing and by how much? Is the financing adequate or inadequate? What are the strengths and weaknesses of the staff and the volunteers? Can their competency, capacity, "clout," and level of involvement be estimated? Is the physical plant adequate? How urgent is expansion or repair? What are the priorities for replacement or additions? Analyzing these factors requires introspection on the part of the institution; it must subject itself to a searching internal examination.

An organization's "audit" must also assess external factors. It should analyze the sociological components of the community, i.e., demographics, power structures, and ethnological and racial composition. Which institutions are leaders in the community? Which are the most prestigious? Where does the library stand in relation to them? How adequate is its location? These are only a few of the more important points an organizational audit should consider. It is a good place for the development effort to begin. Planning starts with facts, since facts are necessary to establish priorities.

A second duty of the development officer is budgeting. A good development person must be a capable budgeter of both time and money. It is imperative that a nonprofit institution be able to justify to its donors and its constituents every dollar raised, every dollar spent, and most certainly, every dollar spent to raise a dollar. Our donors are entitled to hold our institutions to high and exacting standards of accountability, and to scrutinize our efforts.

A tight control on the development budget is essential. Every project should be carefully and separately budgeted, and deemed financially feasible before being undertaken. Every project should be closely monitored so that the budget remains viable. If budgeting realities make a project unfeasible, either the plan must be revised or an alternative project substituted. Decisions to continue or to abort a project based on financial feasibility are extremely difficult, but are the true test of the judgment of the development professional.

The third area of responsibility of the development officer is personnel, administration, and record keeping. All administrators must, of course, have the ability to recognize talent and hire the most able person for any given job. Some of the best and most qualified people can be found among the organization's volunteers — people who are already committed to the institution, who are familiar with it, and who frequently have developed appropriate special skills. Development officers should be both aware of the potential of the volunteers for staff positions, and willing to help those interested and qualified to make the transition. Certain administrative functions require special skills of the development officer. He or she must be able to inspire loyalty to the institution and motivate people to give the extra effort frequently needed to maximize the achievements of the institution. These tasks present unique challenges to the development department. Special events of a developmental nature often require people who can take on unfamiliar projects and work erratic hours. A benefit or fund-raising event may even require herculean efforts on the part of the entire staff. A development director who can achieve the necessary flexibility and motivation within his or her staff so that it can adapt to these demands is invaluable to an organization.

Communication with other departments is an important administrative responsibility. Although the development department may be excluded from operational activities, it cannot afford to exclude the operation departments from developmental functions. Every person in the organization is a development person; every contact with the community, by anyone in the organization, has implications for the institution. It is important to maintain close contact with people throughout the library. Every department should know what the development department is doing and be involved whenever possible. Ultimately, these people are the institution's best publicity agents. They should be involved in all special events, luncheons, photo sessions, and publications. It is axiomatic that the development officer will always want to include as many people as possible, as often as possible, in anything he or she does.

Record keeping may be a tedious responsibility, but it is crucial to know when things happened, how, and to whom. It is completely unacceptable not to know the correct spelling of a donor's name, his title, the amount of his last contribution, or any other important information about a board member or a major donor. Development officers are information specialists, and the more relevant information they can muster, the more effectively they perform. Computers have given us a vast capability for compiling and processing records of donor/member information with a minimum of effort; this whole area of the development function is becoming highly specialized. But whether an organization uses sophisticated computers or three-by-five-inch cards, record keeping is an integral part of the development function and deserves tender loving care.

Fund raising often focuses on specific goal-oriented projects. These can generally be classified as annual operating campaigns, capital campaigns, and long-range or deferred-giving campaigns. Most large, nonprofit institutions have at least an annual campaign and deferred-giving program. A capital campaign may be necessary periodically, although many development officers will never have to manage one. Most organizations turn their capital fund raising over to outside fund-raising consulting firms if capital funds are required.

In the field of fund-raising practice, it is useful to distinguish two kinds of fund-raising efforts — donor acquisition and donor renewal — and the methods that are appropriate to each. Direct mail is the solicitation device used most often for donor acquisition. Personal solicitation and personalized mail are the most common methods used for donor renewal. Special events are appropriate for reaching potential new donors and recommitting former donors. When all the components of development come together in the proper way at the proper time, the result is a charitable contribution — and the development professional must be acutely aware of each of the factors which ultimately achieve this result.

It is a fund raiser's axiom that people give to people. The cause is often a secondary consideration. In the context of a capital campaign, for example, this means that an organization should enlist the most visible, most important person in the community to be chairman. If he or she agrees, the success of the campaign is practically guaranteed.

This leads to consideration of volunteer development, another subject worthy of a separate seminar. A solid, well-informed, active volunteer corps is the most important asset an institution can develop. Not-for-profit organizations fail without caring people, and they grow and prosper when people care. New volunteers must constantly be involved in every area. As with the capital campaign, effective volunteer development means cultivating the enthusiasm and involvement of community leaders. They will bring untold benefits to a cause. A not-for-profit institution which cannot inspire dedicated volunteers should probably critically reexamine its position and image in the community. The key to a successful volunteer program is to treat the volunteer as a professional. He or she must have meaningful tasks, real responsibility, realistic goals, and a chance to see the results of his or her efforts. Next to planning, volunteer development is the officer's most important activity. If this is effective, it can be the beginning of all good things.

On the public relations side of development work, the most basic component of a good program is a regular newsletter. It provides effective communication with the community and, equally important, within the family, i.e., the development staff and volunteers, as it provides regular reinforcement of the importance of their work. The essence of a good newsletter is lots of names and pictures of people. People like to see their names and their friends' names in print. Furthermore, the visibility of a large number of people connotes activity and, of course, activity draws people.

News releases are also a fundamental part of public relations, but getting them in print is tricky business. City newspaper editors and the broadcast media are bombarded with releases, so it takes an unusual approach to catch their attention. The first step a development officer should take is to get acquainted with the city newspaper editor and the news directors at the broadcast stations. He should find out, if possible, how much interest each one has in the library. Libraries have a particular advantage here because they provide — and probably already have provided — research tools for these people. Above all, news releases should not contain trivia, but only that which is dramatic, informative, or widely pertinent to the community. The development officer should call before sending a news release, or better yet, deliver it personally. The availability of public service announcements on radio and television should not be forgotten. All broadcast stations are required to give a certain amount of time to public service announcements. There is someone who selects these announcements at each station. The development officer should find out who it is and make it a point to meet this person. "PSAs" are there for the asking; the development officer should not forget to ask, or be afraid to ask.

There are two essential publications, in addition to the newsletter, which often end up as the responsibility of the development office: the annual report and the basic descriptive brochure. The annual report contains an audited financial statement. It also usually includes a message from the chairman of the board and the president, and an editorial treatment of the highlights of the year's activities. Photographs and other visual treatments can make this report attractive and lively. The content and appearance of the annual report merit attention, since it is vital for the solicitation of large gifts from foundations and major corporate contributors and is often the organization's first introduction to them.

The basic descriptive brochure should detail the service which the institution provides the community. It can include a history of the organization, a listing of the key staff and volunteers, and pictures of the facility. The keys to a successful brochure are drama, clarity and imagination. It may be money well spent to call on the services of professional advertising people to design and produce the brochure.

In addition to the basic descriptive brochure, special printed pieces can be prepared which address separate aspects of the institution's service or solicit funds for special needs. There is a wide variety of printed material that may be prepared by the public relations staff. I strongly recommend that the same graphic theme be used in all of an organization's printed material; this helps to provide a recognizable identity.

The role of community liaison overlaps with many of the development officer's other activities. Public relations, volunteer activities, fund raising, and publicity all create bonds between the organization and the community. But, in addition, an institution should have a specific community relations program. Staff members should be encouraged to join and participate in various service clubs, and to speak at luncheon meetings, school functions, and to church groups. Lectures and presentations at the library to which the public is invited also have "community liaison" benefits.

Part of a community relations program — and the bottom line for evaluating community liaison activities — is continually to emphasize a positive image of the institution and to develop strong ties between it and the community. If the community feels as though the organization is its organization, then development efforts have been successful. And the success will be evident, not only by the level of support received, but also by the way in which the community as a whole will participate in, and will assume responsibility for, maintaining the library. The value of such support is inestimable, particularly when there are political hurdles to leap. Those who have needed rezoning, or building variances, or have had to "fight city hall," will know exactly what this support can mean.

Since the influence of government agencies is growing and becoming increasingly pervasive, it is crucial that a development officer know his political representatives, local, state, and national. He should know key people at any government agency with which he deals or with which he might have to deal in the future. He should be able to get his calls answered and his letters acknowledged. Government agencies can be best friends or fierce foes. Too often, they are our adversaries. The development officer should be aware of this and prepared. It is the job of the development officer to seek the support and recognition of government agencies and officials at all levels.

Many elements have been touched on in this overview of the development function. Every one of them covers a subject about which books have been written, and in which careers have been established. The relationship between and coordination of development and operations, and of planning and day-to-day activities; the organizational audit as the basis for planning; the budgeting process, administration, personnel work, and record keeping; fund raising, public relations, community and government relations; and volunteer activities — these are the components of the development function which library development specialists should be encouraged to understand. The development professional may not have expertise in all of these areas, but he should have a working knowledge of the components — enough so that he knows where to find the people and information he needs to go further. There are enormous rewards in being part of the growth and success of the institutions which we care about and believe in. Furthermore, institutions are the direct beneficiaries of the fact that such rewards are addictive.

TEM HORWITZ

Leadership Dynamics and the Governing Board of a Library Friends Group

Rather than attempt to lay down hard and fast rules or to set up models for the administration of a library friends group, I would like to share some observations about the structure, functions, and organizational patterns that appear to work best in tax-exempt, not-for-profit organizations. My remarks apply to situations where the friends group is legally empowered as the board of trustees or directors of a corporation; where this group is part of a larger governing body; and where this group is in reality an auxiliary board with limited or no formal power.

Every successful not-for-profit, tax-exempt organization with which I have worked has been blessed with one very strong guiding spirit. This person has usually been either the chairman or president of the friends group, or the executive director of the organization. There is always one person who has a vision, a strong will, and the commitment to see that this vision is translated into a program.

Over time, this function can change heads. In fact, it is common for there to be a seesaw relationship between the executive director of the library and the president of the friends board. When one is very strong, the other tends to be weak. The seesaw ceases to work when the movement stops, when either one of these figures remains in a static, extreme position. A chronically weak director is not likely to be effective in carrying out the directives of the friends group, and an ineffective chairman is unlikely to be able to oversee and to counsel the staff of an organization properly. If either figure is too dominant, the other is made ineffectual.

Board members may be inclined to look on their involvement as side actions, as unofficial, and perhaps even as an arrangement simply for show. These leaders should nonetheless be made aware of their responsibilities as executors of a public trust, and the point may be hard to get across. With no economic involvement in the corporation or financial incentives, friends may be inclined not to be all that serious in their commitment. Ultimately, library friends, like libraries themselves, cannot be evaluated, to the extent that their successes and failures can be seen in simple economic terms. Most members of a friends group, accustomed to making evaluations in such terms, are likely to be unfamiliar with the ambiguities of library programs. The program which is the least cost-effective may be the most significant one that the library provides, and this program will attract future foundation support or, in a less immediate way, create enormous goodwill in the community. Not only do some of these equations become exceedingly complex, but the program evaluation itself may seem like it is taking place on shifting sands. Authority and credibility thus accrue to the leader who (if a few classic metaphors may be used) knows the game plan, is producing the show, and knows where the bodies are buried.

To use a more organic metaphor in describing friends groups, the president, working through the board, functions as the brain while the board, working through the membership, provides the independent functions that are performed by the organism. The group as a whole can be seen as a complex and shifting mixture of skills, interests, commitments, needs, goals, and desires. Given this complexity, without a guiding central intelligence, the group easily becomes an amorphous, conflicted, ineffectual organism. A board, like a well-cared-for bonsai plant, must continually be in the process of being shaped. The organization must always be asking what needs to be done, and who can do it.

It is common to look to friends to provide services the organization needs but is not anxious to pay for, e.g., accounting, design, printing, legal, fund-raising, advertising, architectural, and mailing services. It is a common fallacy for friends groups to seek out a congenial attorney, for instance, who is asked to be part of the group with the assumption that he will provide free legal services for the organization. Make sure that persons asked to join for this reason are actually interested in providing the service. An accountant may be attracted to a friends group mainly because it has nothing to do with accounting. The attorney may be delighted to serve and anxious to provide legal services, but may have no expertise in the kinds of legal problems with which friends groups are faced. The architect may be interested in redesigning the library auditorium, but will be annoyed when expected to work against a deadline. Many donated services are further accompanied with a heavy dose of "beggars can't be choosers." It may actually be cheaper and more efficient to pay for services that are available free from board members.

Members of a friends group are often made board members in the expectation that they will thereby be intimately connected to fund-raising efforts, i.e., they will give money, they will get their friends to give money, they will approach their friends at foundations and corporations for money, and they will organize events which will raise funds for the organization. None of these should be taken for granted. Find out in advance, to the extent possible, what friends are willing and able to do as board members. We know, for generalizations, that people are strange in giving money and in asking other people for it. There are rich folk who are tight with their own money, but delighted to hit their friends on the library's behalf. Others find it extremely painful to ask anything from anybody. Still others can organize fund raising for large numbers of people with no problem. Remember that those with the most money — the obvious marks — are probably oversubscribed already. To anticipate the capabilities of members of a group requires an investment of time, energy, candor, and guile.

One of the most underused skills readily available to nonprofit organizations is that of management. American businessmen have worked out sophisticated ways of operating businesses, managing groups of workers, and making intelligent managerial decisions. Of course, not everyone who is successful in business is a good manager, and not every good manager will be effective in nonprofit work. There is, however, a large and relatively untapped reservoir of skills. Friends from the executive/managerial/business world can provide counsel to the staff, work as troubleshooters within the organization, and even restructure or resolve internal conflicts. A warning is in order, though: it is not uncommon for successful business people, consciously or unconsciously, to look down on managers of nonprofit organizations, viewing them as "sissies" or failed business people who can't make it in the "real" world.

Someone in the friends organization must know what is going on and have a day-to-day involvement in the affairs of the library. Logically, this person might be the library director. The friends group, either as a whole or in the person of its chief officer, must have an intimate knowledge of what is happening, how it is happening, and why it is happening. Someone must be able to see the whole picture, to be in a position to resolve internal problems, and to spot future areas of conflict. However the specific functions are divided, to work effectively the friends group must be potent.

The question remains, "where do board members come from?" Many groups seem hopelessly committed to the search for the rich and the famous, operating under the perhaps unarticulated assumption that the presence of "stars" will somehow miraculously solve the problems of the organization. This is the *deus ex machina* fallacy of board recruitment. As often as not, "stars" are already oversubscribed and underinspired. A better place to start is with friends and friends of friends who have made some contribution to the library. But be careful not to become too exclusively identified with one group or segment of the community. Care must be taken not to discourage from joining other groups that could be helpful, or to create the image of a private club. Figure out what groups, classes, and segments of the public should be represented on your board. Draw up an overall plan and work from it, modifying it as you go along, but avoiding a haphazard selection process.

Someone must be in touch with each of the board members to communicate their decisions, attitudes, and achievements to either a committee or to the central figure on the board. This figure must understand why each of these individuals has agreed to be on the board, what they feel they can contribute, exactly what they are willing to do, and what they want from their involvement with the library. And this is tricky. Board members may talk about how important the library is to the community, but really be interested only in the points they hope to score from being on the board. Others may talk of civic responsibility, but feel that they have to serve on friends groups because their father and grandfather did; it is expected of those in their family. A member may want an arena in which to exercise some power. Persons may be driven by guilt because they have made so much money; they may be bored with their lives; or they may have a genuine need to serve. None of these motives is necessarily bad, but whatever the motivations, someone must understand them, must collect from each friend what he or she has to give and what the organization needs, while also providing for the personal needs and fulfilling the expectations of each member of the friends group.

The relationship between the head of the friends group or the director and the members of the friends group must of necessity be intimate, requiring someone who is a diligent student of human nature. This leader must be cunning, flexible, exacting, and generous — a Machiavellian figure or a Confucian gentleman.

Over time, even those board members who are most active and interested in the library will tend to become bored or less energetic. It is highly desirable to have terms of service. A year is usually too short, five years too long; two- to three-year terms are usually best. Overlapping terms are desirable to keep the board from changing over completely at one time. Old friends who have done their service, but who still do an occasional favor or who have a special contact, may be usefully honored by appointment to an advisory group or auxiliary board. This group can exist only on your letterhead, or it can meet over tea and discuss old times; it can even be an active functioning group in its own right.

The size of the board depends on a number of factors: how much there is to do, the internal dynamics of the group, and optimum working size. A group of six, for example, might be too small, too close, too boring. On the other hand, a group of thirty might be too diffuse, too impersonal, too unwieldy. There are no hard and fast rules, and the right solution at one time will change over the years. An additional consideration is the style of the president of the group. Some people are superb in work with groups of five or six, but totally ineffective at running a meeting with twenty-five people. Other leaders are in their element with large groups, but wrong in small groups — their gaze is too lofty; they project too far into the room; their manner is excessive for the nature of the contacts.

Board meetings must be scheduled often enough so that the work gets done, and so that there is a sense of continuing involvement. If there are too many meetings, participation will be a burden. Too few meetings will give a feeling of discontinuity. Such matters must be worked out for each group and each organization. If there seems to be too much to get through at each meeting, have more frequent meetings or have the issues flushed out in smaller and (one hopes) more efficient committees.

Auxiliary boards may prove useful in organizing special events, providing specific services, and generally taking pressure off of the friends group itself. In addition, such boards can be a proving ground for future board members of the friends group, a retirement home for former board members, a platform for figureheads, and a not-dishonorable dumping ground for failed experiments.

A productive and successful friends group is the product of innumerable relationships, contacts, and activities. It is a system in which each of the components somehow fuels the others over time, generating programs and new activities, reaching a larger body of people, and producing a continually enlarging series of contacts and potential activities. When all of the pieces are properly assembled, activities seem to grow out of each other, magically and seemingly without effort. When the organization, for whatever reason, is on the wrong track, the simplest activities seem to require enormous expenditures of energy to go no place.

Meanwhile, tensions often arise between the library staff, the administration, and the friends group. At worst, the friends group looks on the administration as dull hacks; the administration looks at the friends group as a necessary evil to be tolerated and manipulated; and the staff sees both groups as being out of touch with the day-to-day realities of the library. When communication under such conditions tends to be poor, the friends group is generally unproductive and not well organized. The administration in turn feels resentful because there is no sustained involvement on the part of the friends.

The model for the nonprofit organizations comes largely from the profit-making corporations which are founded and often run by strong, tough, hard-nosed, John Wayne-type individualists. The strengths and weaknesses of this model are refracted when they are translated from the corporate to the nonprofit world. Strong leadership is essential; but there is also another model which complements and balances it, derived from the experience of many in my own generation working in collectives of varying sorts. My limited understanding of the organization of Japanese business suggests that one sees it there as well. This model is one of consensus. It is built on the premise that every member of the group will have a veto power which can be exercised at any time with respect to any decision of the organization. This veto can be either an explicit right, or simply an unstated working principle. For those of us on the outside, used to majority rule, it looks pretty scary. In practice, the exercise of the veto places a very heavy responsibility on anyone who would choose to exercise it — except perhaps the inveterate troublemaker. In my experience, though, every time a veto has been used, there has been good reason, some problem to which the rest of the group was not as sensitive. Group pressure tends to discourage the use of the veto. The veto right creates and assures a feeling of solidarity: all of the group decisions have the force and commitment of the whole group behind them. The limitation of the model is a certain built-in slowness. A time-consuming process is called for, one which requires patience as well as the development of a certain kind of grace, which is generally lacking in much of our socialized behavior.

In conclusion, these points regarding the board seem to be in order:

1. The board members should be effective individually in their work.
2. They should have complementary talents.
3. They should be representative of the interests served by the organization.
4. The board should be large enough to get all of the work done, but small enough to be intimate.
5. There should be clear organizational patterns and good communication between the board and the library staff.
6. It is essential to have good working relationships among the board, the staff, and the organization's executive.
7. The board should have a total sense of the organization's objectives.
8. The board should know to what degree these objectives are being realized by the organization.
9. The members should be comfortable with one another.
10. Each member should feel involved with the work of the board and the progress of the organization.
11. The board should have specific goals.
12. The board should make policy decisions only after talking to all concerned parties; it should not operate in a vacuum.
13. The board should enjoy good relations with its community.
14. Members should derive a sense of achievement from their board work.

CYNTHIA WEDEL

The Management of Volunteers

Volunteers can and should be an important part of every nonprofit organization. This is not only to save money — though it can do that — but because it is a right of people to have an active share in those institutions which are supported by their tax or philanthropic dollars. The volunteer portion of our society is undergoing some dramatic changes today which offer new challenges and many new opportunities to all organizations which are alert to what is happening. I don't know a great deal about the detailed operations of libraries (although I worked in one at one time), but the basic principles of volunteer participation and management, I am sure, apply to libraries as they do to hospitals, school systems, and social welfare agencies.

To understand these changes, we must look at what is happening to people today which has an effect on volunteering. First of all, people now are far better educated than earlier generations and very much better informed. Indeed, the mass media bring most of us an overload of information with an unfortunate emphasis on the tragic or sensational. However, one good result is that most people are aware — as earlier generations could not be — of needs and opportunities which exist in their community, the nation, and the world, and the normal human reaction to a need is, "I wish I could do something to help."

Second, people today have far more discretionary time than people of earlier days. (I have learned never to call this "leisure" time. Americans seem to have enough remnants of the old work ethic to be very defensive about leisure.) But compared with even a half-century ago, when the normal workweek was six days of ten to twelve hours (eighteen hours for farmers and housewives), all of us today have far more time to use as we may choose.

Third, an amazing number of people spend their working hours at routine, unfulfilling jobs. Studies have shown that the number of people who find their daily work very satisfying is shockingly small. Almost everyone has interests and potential talents which he or she has little or no opportunity to develop.

All of this means that every town and city has many, many people who are concerned about the community, have time available, and have a great deal of untapped potential. Unfortunately, many of us are so hung up on old notions about volunteers and volunteer work that we are unaware of these facts. To most people, the word *volunteer* conjures up the mental image of a middle-aged, middle-class housewife, with no specific skills, but with a warm heart and quite a bit of free time. We think of her working as a volunteer a day or two each week in a hospital or welfare agency.

But, as we all realize, the middle-aged, middle-class housewife is an endangered species. Today's housewife is probably going to work or back to school, or is in demand by every agency in town. This is why so many people today are talking and writing about the decline in volunteering. There is no such decline. On the contrary, there is an explosion of volunteering which is unprecedented since the day of the early colonists, when everyone had to volunteer to provide housing, education, health care, and aid to those in trouble.

Much of the growth in voluntary activity is seen in the many "cause" groups which spring up to fight the freeway, secure better housing, or meet some other local problem. Volunteer bureaus and voluntary action centers in most towns and cities receive many calls from people who want to volunteer — and sometimes there are not enough jobs available. While there is still a good solid volunteer corps of traditional housewives, their ranks are being expanded by working men and women eager to give time and skill if it can be done after work or on weekends. Young people today are an excellent source of volunteers: they are aware of needs, eager to help, and often find volunteer work a way to gain experience and try out career possibilities.

Probably the richest source of new volunteer power, however, is the rapidly growing group of retirees. People today retire earlier, are healthier, and live longer than those in the past. For many, the greatest problem is boredom and feeling unwanted and unneeded. We are also discovering many competent volunteers among the physically disabled. There are plenty of volunteers. If we begin to accept and believe this, and undertake the recruitment of volunteers with a positive rather than negative approach, we will succeed.

There are a number of things we need to know, however, before we can launch a volunteer program or expand the one we have. First of all, we need to recognize that there are three basic types of volunteers, all of which can be very useful. There are the "policy-making" volunteers, those who are members of boards or committees. They need to be carefully chosen and helped to do a constructive and satisfying job. People today, for the most part, resent being used as "rubber stamps." They will be active and helpful if they are given a real chance to do so. This means that they should be told, when asked to serve, that they will be expected to work. The board should have working committees, and every member should be involved in one. The board chairman may need help in learning to use committees well. When decisions must be made, the chairman and staff executive should be sure that everyone has the necessary information and that, as far as possible, several alternatives are offered for their discussion and decision. It is equally annoying to a board to be offered one course of action and told to vote "yes" or "no," as to be faced with a difficult problem with no possible solutions suggested.

A second — and very important — type of volunteer is the "management" volunteer. If eight volunteers are needed to do a particular task, look first for a capable person to act as chairperson, "captain," or manager of that particular work force, and then, with his or her help, round up the others. Spend enough time with the chairperson to make sure that he or she thoroughly understands what is to be done. Then assign that person the task of training, scheduling, and supervising the others.

Many overworked staff people, in any kind of agency, tend to resist the idea of using volunteers because they imagine being faced with eight or ten eager people asking, "What do you want me to do?" The idea of finding specific jobs for them, showing them how to do the jobs, answering their questions, listening to their complaints, and finally checking on their work is so overwhelming that the staff person usually decides to wait until later. Here the administrative volunteer is the solution. He or she needs to be carefully selected and must be a responsible and reasonably well organized person. You may have a friend who fits this category, or you may know someone who has recently retired, or there may be a good candidate on some of your boards or committees. Most communities have housewives or retired people who have been librarians or have had library training. You might set up a small committee of volunteers on your board who would help find the right person.

There are a surprising number of potential volunteers who want to work with people rather than with things — like books or file cards. Enlisting, training, helping, and supervising a group of volunteers would appeal to such a person. Voluntary groups in your community, such as a volunteer bureau, voluntary action center, the Red Cross, the Junior League, church groups, or service clubs, would help you locate such a person, or perhaps two people. In a couple of hours you could explain your needs, introduce them to the library and its program and, you hope, get their commitment to help.

Such a chairman of volunteers would be responsible for recruiting, training, assigning, assisting, and evaluating the work of volunteers. As a staff person, you would be in the background to answer questions, but the day-to-day work can be done by volunteers. You should be able to get the help you need, with a minimum of additional work on your part.

The third echelon of volunteers is the "service volunteer," the one who does the actual job. You may need help with cataloging and shelving books, or at the reception or check-out desk. You may want someone to be responsible for periodicals or a reading room. You might want a volunteer to conduct story-hours for children or a program of reading to the blind. If you get a group of volunteers involved, they will themselves come up with new and imaginative ideas for services which the library might offer.

To make volunteer work attractive and satisfying to people today, there are several things which need to be done. First, the board and other staff must really want volunteers. They must understand that volunteers can help expand services, make the library better known and more appreciated in the community, and help win greater support.

Second, with the help of at least one experienced volunteer, you need to decide what you want done, and then design the various tasks to be done by part-time workers because most volunteers can only provide part-time help. This means job descriptions — simple and nontechnical, but specific and clear (again, a large voluntary organization like the Red Cross would be happy to share samples of volunteer job descriptions). There is nothing which gives a potential volunteer a better feeling for a place than the realization that staff know what they want, and can express it clearly in writing. Remember that most volunteers today have had business experience and are accustomed to things like job descriptions.

It is a good idea to enter into a simple "contract" with the volunteer whereby he or she agrees to give a specific amount of time and to do the specified job. You, in turn, agree to provide the needed training and supervision, and inform the volunteer about where to go for help. It is wise if you or the volunteer chairman, after a certain period of time — a month or three months — sit down with the volunteer and assess how things are working out. This gives you a normal, nonthreatening chance to suggest needed improvements in the volunteer's performance, and gives the volunteer the opportunity to express satisfaction or dissatisfaction, to make suggestions, or to ask for an additional or different assignment.

For most volunteers, an interesting job providing needed help is enough reward. But some planned recognition can be meaningful, not only to the volunteer, but as a device for recruiting more volunteers. Most volunteers say that the best recognition is a sincere "thank you" from staff, or a spontaneous "I don't know what we would do without you." But, perhaps once a year, some formal recognition is excellent public relations. It might be a luncheon, tea, or dinner with certificates of appreciation to the volunteers. Or it might be an "open house" at the library, with special exhibits and a brief recognition ceremony.

A full-blown volunteer program doesn't appear overnight. It is far better to move slowly, taking on just one or two volunteers at a time. But over a period of two or three years the benefits can be great. More and better service can be provided. Public relations can be greatly improved. Indeed, it is often possible to find a volunteer with public relations skill and experience who can plan and carry out a program of ongoing information and interpretation of the work and the services which the library offers. As citizens of the community become personally involved in the library, they begin to realize that it really is *theirs*. And all of us will work to support, strengthen, and expand that which really belongs to us.

MARIANNE G. BRISCOE

Library Friends Groups and Their "Perquisites"

Although the benefits offered to library friends or regular donors are often called "perquisites" ("perks" for short), the term is troublesome when it implies that the goods, services, or privileges offered in exchange for an annual payment are justly due the donor. Managers of library friends groups who view benefits as "just deserts" may not take advantage of their full potential. Instead of wondering what a library benefactor deserves in exchange for a contribution, we ought to look for the best use we can make of an opportunity to give something to a regular donor. We need to ponder how to make an advantage out of what is frequently viewed as an obligation.

In most cases library friends groups are created to help support a library's operating budget through fund raising, to disseminate information about a library, and to foster goodwill in the community. And while the benefits and gifts offered to supporters should express gratitude, they should also be wisely designed to help achieve some of the library's goals in establishing and sustaining an effective friends group.

The goals for a friends group naturally include the contribution of unrestricted annual gifts, one hopes in quantity, to support book purchase funds or the operating budget. But such a group is also a magnet for new supporters, serving as an open, easily accessible, clearly explained way of giving money to a library to help with its work. Through membership recruitment efforts, friends groups can create important, high-quality publicity, while individual members provide access to power and influence in the community. Finally, and most important, a friends group can be the means to upgrade modest or casual donors to leaders of trustee caliber, or to bring these people to the status of major institutional benefactors through bequests, trusts and annuities, or major lifetime gifts.

In short, an effective friends group is not only a money-raising endeavor. Equally important, it is an interest-raising and interest-sustaining enterprise. And, one should be calculating: a "perk" should be offered to stimulate a friend's generosity to, or his interest in, the library. Keep in mind that if the friend is not interested in your library he will not make a gift; if he does give, most of the time he is signaling that he wants to be further informed about you.

While it is wise to be competitive with other libraries, museums, or cultural institutions when drawing up a benefit package, it is wiser still to make sure that the "perks" offered will communicate your library's special character. Let them be more than appropriate to the image of your institution; make them apt.

This means that before you decide what "perks" to offer, you must determine what it is about the library that interests your donors. In the friends business it is likely that, in some shape or form, the primary interest is books. After that the problem becomes more difficult; the interests vary from institution to institution and among donors. Your library's special appeal may be its role in research support to a college or university; its status as a conveyor of library services and information to the reading public, to children, or to the disadvantaged; or that it has an important collection on a subject of interest, such as genealogy or seventeenth-century English literature.

Once the particular appeal of your library is identified, you must then decide what your friends are like, or could or should be like. This does not mean asking how wealthy they are at the outset; one almost never knows a library friend's giving capacity. On an absolute scale a $15 or a $150 annual gift — often, in the library's view, the difference between an ordinary and a special donor — may not be indicative of the donor's wealth. That $15 may be less than 1 percent of his total giving; the $150 may represent 90 percent of his annual gifts to charity. Furthermore, the actual wealth of a friend, at least at the beginning of his membership, has little to do with the amount he gives. His first gifts are made to become one of your donors, to get his name on the list, to establish membership, but not to endow or sustain your operations. But from little acorns grow mighty oaks. Eventually, if the friends group effectively motivates generosity and interest, the wealth of some friends will become obvious and, over time, with the proper cultivation, they may move beyond the realm of benefits and memberships to the status of VIP donors and very good friends.

In establishing a profile of your library's friends, consider first what classes of interest they represent, and how they came to be friends. The most obvious category of friends includes current and former readers. They know the library very well, probably both its strengths and weaknesses, and they may have followed its activities for a long time. In general, this is the least wealthy category of donors; and given the well-established view that library access is an American birthright paid for through taxes or tuitions, this can be the hardest group to persuade that *they* ought to support their library.

But to earn anyone else's support — corporate, governmental, foundation, or personal — you ought to prove that your patrons value the library enough to contribute. A second group of friends includes tourists, visitors, and people who view your exhibitions, attend your public programs, or use your facilities for meetings or other events. This might be regarded as the casual trade in the library. There is probably also a group of "nonreaders" who believe in libraries. These people often collect books themselves or they may, for personal or historical reasons, be particularly attached to your library. Generally, this is the wealthiest and most generous class of friend. Finally, there are community leaders who routinely support good cultural causes. These people may be politicians, socialites, or business and professional people. Their wealth will vary greatly, as will their interest in your library's work.

A second important characteristic of friends is the extent of their actual contact with your library. Are they locals who frequent the neighborhood and can be counted on to view exhibitions or attend events? Do they live in Europe, or on a far coast? Or are they of a profession or disposition that makes them unlikely, though they live nearby, to take advantage of social offerings?

A friends group may be all of one or the other sort, but this is unlikely if there has been a good member recruitment effort. Therefore, a package of benefits must appeal both to the "foreigners" and "locals" in the membership. And any one "perk" will do well to appeal to several classes of friends at once. Furthermore, the good benefit offering, like the Horatian ode, should have as its end instruction and delight: its goals are to provoke interest in your library and generosity to it.

Of the several classes of friends just outlined, the ones most reliable, potentially generous, and responsive to "perks" will probably come from two groups: the current and former readers who know the institution but may not be very sophisticated or charitable givers and the nonreaders who like the library because it is an important charity in the community, who like what the library is doing, or who have some other personal reason for their interest. So, if the goal is to develop benefits that reach the most people who can do the most good for your library, you now know who your "perks" audience is.

Perquisites can instruct and delight these people with descriptions of your book collections and materials, or of your research, education, and community service activities. You can give them inside acquaintance with aspects of library business that are of special interest to the layman, such as a conservation or binding project, or a subject of widespread interest, like genealogy. You can have them help celebrate a particular triumph, such as the acquisition of an important collection, the receipt of a special award by your library, or a library-related award or accomplishment of a staff member; or enlist them to observe special events in the library's history. Always choose events and gifts which will say in a discreet, nonverbal manner that a special and enlightened class of people support the library, people with whom friends should be pleased to associate either socially, as at receptions and lectures, or as a name on a list of honored donors.

As friends become more knowledgeable about your library, the exigencies of your financial situation may come to interest them. Then the race is nearly won, because in the dynamics of a library friends group, the act of giving should become a "perk" in itself. Your best friends will become interested in the library's welfare rather than in their own rewards. Friends can then be encouraged to furnish a room for the library; to sustain a special outreach or research program; to buy a book that is expensive, rare, or beautiful and especially desired by the library; to run a volunteer program or a bookshop or docents program; or to help meet a challenge grant to recruit new friends. Afterward they can join in celebrating their generosity with a special public event or publication that is more commonly recognized as a "perk" or benefit.

By now it should be clear that I favor receptions, dinners, exhibitions and exhibition openings, lectures, concerts and other performances, newsletters, calendars, keepsake and commemorative publications, special appeals, and sponsored tours. Bookshop discounts, special lending or other library privileges seem less appropriate as friends benefits (though if your competition offers them you may have to follow suit) because they are relatively passive offerings. You are not engaging the attention and goodwill of a friend on behalf of the library with bookshop discounts. In the case of lending privileges, you are bordering on a contractual relationship with a donor that may seem to compromise your free library status in the view of your general readers (though in truth that may not be the case). Such an offering may take the edge off the *generosity-invoking* nature of the relationship you want to foster.

Once you have a general sense of the appropriate perquisites, how do you assure that the ones you choose are "cost-effective"? This, of course, is one of the hardest questions to answer. You can determine how much benefit offerings cost, and you will know how much money you raise through the friends group in a fiscal year. That may give a rough estimate of the effectiveness of your offerings from year to year. But given the other factors involved in friends' giving, that is a rather crude measure of effectiveness. Furthermore, "perks" are offered in order to find, to keep, and to develop friendships; and from that perspective their cost-effectiveness must be viewed over a longer term than one or three fiscal years.

A better measure of effectiveness may well be the number of members. If enrollment is declining or if the renewal rate is poor (be aware that a renewal rate of only 80 percent is not uncommon, especially in the wake of a membership drive), you ought to evaluate your offerings in a colder light. If you hold events and only a fraction of your friends attend, it is time to retrench. And if you make a special appeal and get little or no response, look to the nature of your appeal, your publicity, *and* the kinds of things you are giving your members.

The cost of a "perk" is frequently easy to determine; it is far more difficult to assess its value and impact. There is one certain factor in evaluating a benefit: a shabby or otherwise second-class offering simply should not be made. It is better to make the main benefit of membership the federal income tax deduction available to the charitable giver than to pain a donor with a less than competent offering. Remember, everything given a donor as a benefit is, in the eyes of the Internal Revenue Service, a reduction of his charitable gift. If membership costs $10 and the friend gets $6 in benefits, the IRS may only let the donor count $4 as a charitable gift. The value of the benefits offered in exchange for membership in charitable associations is a frequent focus of discussion among donors, donees and tax men.

Another caveat: make the highest priority "perks" those that reach the greatest number of friends. Most obviously, do a newsletter — of high quality editorially, but not lavish. And be sure that its content hews to the instruct-and-delight, motivate-and-recognize theme. Consider offering an occasional keepsake publication or, an application especially suited to libraries, a calendar based on illustrated books and other materials in your collections. If you are lucky they will hang it on a wall by the phone and think of you every day.

By all means have offerings that get friends into your building, into the presence of your senior or most interesting staff and readers, into the interesting business of the library, and into the presence of one another. Give those who like belonging, in addition to supporting, a sense of the friends as more than a bank account for the library's benefit. Exhibition openings are an easy and natural way to do this. Occasionally (once a year may be sufficient) have an event, widely publicized, for friends only. It should make the membership realize again with pleasure that your library is a place for learning, with enough influence in the intellectual community to bring important, learned, or famous people to speak or perform for them. This is often expensive, though not necessarily so; but it will have a major impact, when properly publicized, not only on those members who attend, but on those who did not attend, and on your all-important *potential* membership.

In sum, benefits offered to annual donors should be an important part of an overall strategy for accomplishing the goals of a friends group. It takes a lot of work to run such a group, and the "perks" substantially increase the labor and expense. So take care to use your resources of time, money, and energy in an efficient and productive manner. This means that if you see your friends group as a fund- and support-raising arm of your library, membership in the friends group should be marketed on the basis of helping a great library to grow and to remain great — or some such high-minded goal. Allude to perquisite offerings, but do not use them as a primary selling point. Then offer perquisites that are attractive to new donors, that make regular donors feel good about belonging, and that are designed to entertain members while instructing them about your library in a manner that will increase their concern for your welfare and financial stability. This is no small task, but "perks" are an excellent device for sustaining your annual budget and paving the way for larger gifts by recruiting and cultivating donors at the entry level. In these days of shrinking foundation and personal fortunes, the support of the multitudes, despite the high costs of getting and keeping it, is essential to the survival of cultural institutions like libraries.

WILLIAM R. HOLMAN

Library Friends Publications

W ell-designed graphics and printing are essential for friends publications. In our service to both the library and the community, we stress the need for enlisting the most able and imaginative friends for our endeavors. We look for friends with knowledge and discrimination in expressing the library's various programs, services, and purposes. Any publication issued by the friends should reflect a warmth and grace that will motivate public interest and response for both the library and the friends. Aldous Huxley has said that "good printing can create a valuable spiritual state in the reader," the very state which we hope will promote increased receptiveness to the various projects sponsored by the friends.

It is not uncommon for members of a friends organization to spend weeks or even months in analyzing, planning, and preparing lengthy annual reports, newsletters, and other publications. The investment is considerable; resulting publications should not be issued in a banal or unattractive manner. The cost of issuing a fine publication is little more than that of a mediocre one. It is merely a matter of type and graphic design, the selection of appropriate paper, and the careful use of illustrations. Today, it is practical for friends groups to produce publications at reasonable costs. Almost all libraries — public, college, school, or university — have at their disposal an offset duplicator, either located in the city, county, school, or college offices, or available through a local printer. Once the copy has been properly typeset, an overall design executed, and camera-ready copy prepared, any piece can be printed attractively on a limited budget.

Let us think briefly about the aesthetics of design in their broadest aspects and the importance this holds for each of us. Design surrounds us at every turn. Daily our eyes perceive thousands of objects: buildings, automobiles, street lamps, desks, chairs, clothing. Some of the most important, however, are those objects which communicate a message to us: signs, advertisements, newspapers, books, leaflets, broadsides, annual reports, and newsletters. These printed pieces can be written and designed to evoke satisfaction and pleasure to our senses; or they can be executed so thoughtlessly that they offend our eye and our intelligence.

For background, it is invaluable to examine critically, and to learn to take pleasure in, letter forms, books, paper, and binding as seen in examples of fine bookmaking. The sources of our modern-day standards go back to ancient Rome. In the excavated Roman ruins at Bath, England, for example, one can already see fullness and width on the body of letters; serifs appear at the beginning and end of almost all of them. These letter forms possess a grace and beauty in their own right which call for no further embellishment or decoration; each letter stands as a work of art.

During the Renaissance, the Roman ideal was kept alive in the work of Aldus Manutius, the great Venetian printer and scholar. Aldus was most careful to place small pieces of spacing material between each of the capital letters used for chapter headings. This has a distinct purpose: it makes the roman capital letters more readable since the lead spaces, each about the width of the letter *i*, give light value. They keep the letters from crowding each other and becoming difficult to read. In the text itself, however, the words are generally set very close to one another. They are not driven apart by excessive spacing which results in "rivers of light" running down through the printed page.

The type page itself is well proportioned and properly placed toward the optical left side of the sheet; the margins are liberal, giving a pleasing contrast between the text and the page. There is a solid visual feeling in the mass of type on the page, since each line is closely situated to the other. The use of very modest spacing between the lines is possible with Latin, which has few ascender and descender letters in its text matter.

It is equally important to look at the work of John Baskerville, the eighteenth-century English printer. In the title page of his great Bible of 1763, one sees evidence of his early training as a writing master and stone carver. The words printed in capital letters are letterspaced: light value has been added between each letter as well as between each word. Some critics feel that the letterspacing is excessive, but it does make the words more legible. Bypassing William Morris, perhaps the best-known figure of the Crafts Revival, we should look instead to the Doves Press, founded in 1900 by T.J. Cobden-Sanderson and Emery Walker. Unlike Morris, they believed in the beauty of perfect proportion. They sought neither brilliance nor magnificence, but rather a lucidity achieved through clean, well-spaced type, simply arranged. In their approach, ornament and splendor were irrelevant. To my taste, the Doves Bible represents the greatest work in twentieth-century fine bookmaking, with its closely set type, classic margins, and clean beauty of the page. Today we should keep in mind the simple elegance of their restrained yet richly pleasing work. Equally valuable books to examine are the works of the Ashendene Press; Updike's *Book of Common Prayer,* restrained and warm in its execution; or the Grabhorn *Leaves of Grass.*

Recognized as one of the dozen or so greatest books produced in America, this is one whose text I had never read until I read this edition.

The world of books, however, is but one manifestation of our encounter with the graphic world. That which surrounds us in our everyday life — the streets and shops which dominate graphic expression in America — present colors that are garish, letter forms that are mostly sans-serif or that have serifs of the Egyptian variety from English typographical design. The letter forms are often distorted; they shout rather than speak intelligibly and with clarity. In the typical American automobile row today, even the salesmen show that they have lost confidence in their signs: they resort to the use of plastic pennants and pinwheels. Thus, poor graphics and ill-conceived letter forms can be a blight which effectively destroy the unity of our surroundings, when by rights they should help to enhance it. In contrast, Ghirardelli Square in San Francisco offers contemporary commercial developments on the west coast. Formerly a red-brick factory building for the processing of chocolate, it now houses a complex of small business firms. The design of its signs and various graphics creates a visual delight. Here one sees, for instance, sans-serif letters combined on a sign with simple structural lines, its stiffness softened by a subtle orange border, thus blending elements of the building; natural woods utilized with a nineteenth-century ornate letter, combining to make a warm and appealing graphic sign; an old English-type coffee house signboard utilizing gold-leaf roman letters with fine serifs, combining dignity and restraint with a touch of elegance; or elsewhere, Egyptian-style letters distinguished by square serifs, their simplicity adding grace and beauty to rather bold letter forms, so as to be able to stand by themselves without embellishment. Here, in sum, one sees letter forms used with taste and harmony, to add delight to man's everyday ventures.

From such books, and other uses of letter forms, we can understand some rather broad standards to follow in printing for the friends and for the library.

First, we should strive for good proportion in the interrelationship of type, illustrations, and margins. Good proportion does not mean that all masses of type must be equal, nor that a page must have the same size illustrations at the top and at the bottom. Instead, an interesting variation of shapes and blocks of type is more pleasing.

Symmetry is another principle of design which should be considered. Most printed pieces fall into one of the two distinct forms of design. In the classical or traditional type of design, everything is symmetrical and suggestive of rest. The point of balance is usually in the optical center of the design. This is found by dividing the area into two vertical halves by drawing a line down the middle and marking off the optical center at a point approximately one-third the distance from the top of the line. The opposite of symmetrical design is the asymmetrical arrangement, which places the elements of typography in an off-center arrangement — particularly as they relate to the vertical axis of the page. This is often the more modernistic approach, and must be handled with considerable judgment and care. Otherwise it will not provide relief from the formal or traditional balanced approach.

Several words of advice are in order regarding the use of typefaces. Make an effort to combine no more than two in any one printed page. Variety can be obtained, instead, through the use of capital letters or small capitals, capital letters combined with small capitals, and/or italic capitals and lower case combined with roman upper-case letters. In order to be effective, type should not shout, but should speak to you in an evenly modulated voice. If you desire a strong statement, use a well-designed type such as Goudy's Hadriano, Hermann Zapf's Sistina, or others constructed in the best tradition of fine letter forms. Avoid eccentric or grotesque type, as it seldom equals the better types and usually lends an unwelcome feeling to any printed piece. When in doubt, use such standard forms as Janson, Garamond, Caslon, Times Roman, Palatino, Sabon, Caledonia, Primer, and similar roman faces. Type should be set, in general, no longer than twelve to fifteen words per line. Use adequate margins in the gutter, the head, the outer edges, and the foot. Remember that the printed page should be designed to be held in the hand, so leave enough room in the outer margins for the thumb to take hold of the page. Set as much text as possible in roman lower-case letters; try to avoid all capital letters. When a few words are set in all capitals for a chapter heading, make certain that each word is optically letterspaced for ease in reading; this must be specified on your copy. Also specify close spacing between words; be mindful of rivers of light running down through your copy. Generally, set your copy in 10- or 12-point type, with two points of leading between each line. Caledonia is readable in 10-point size set on a 12-point body; 11-point type is even more readable.

When you select a paper, make an effort to utilize an off-white natural paper which isn't coated (with a glossy surface). A wove-finish, eggshell, off-white colored paper is most friendly to the type and the eye. When specifying ink, avoid the temptation to be clever; merely specify a black ink for your copy. If you wish a decorative effect, use a terra-cotta red for a single word or heading. If you don't care for the often-used red ink, utilize a blue softened with a tint of gray.

Finally, avoid the use of office, city, and university seals. They are usually copied from one another, and are too often uninspired, listless, unimaginative, and difficult to read. Search out other devices, or have an artist create a logo for your printed work.

Successful use of these several principles of design requires planning, broken down here into four major steps:

1. Establish the objectives for the printed piece. Your copy will follow more naturally. Who is the audience and what do you desire to accomplish? You shouldn't speak down, and you shouldn't be clever. If one member of the friends group is blessed with the ability to write lucid prose, recruit this person to write the copy.

2. Design the publication in a penciled layout of how the final printed piece will appear. This requires that the copy be "cast off," that is, that the total number of typed characters be counted off from the manuscript copy. This total number of typewritten characters should be fitted to the design as it will appear in printed type. At this stage, the paper, the size, and the dimensions — usually allow for a quarter-inch trim — need to be established, and a dummy prepared.

3. Set the type and gather the illustrations. The type should be specified on the manuscript copy in the upper right-hand corner, i.e., the name of the typeface to be used, its size, the leading between the lines, and the length of the type line in pica measurement.

   If your friends group must set its publication on a typewriter, it is often wise to use an IBM Composer, which gives excellent results for the investment. One of the better typefaces available is Baskerville. Setting copy in 11- or 12-point size and then reducing it by 5 percent will sharpen the copy. Make an effort to keep the copy above 10-point size, however. If your group desires a quality publication, on the other hand, it is better to have the type set, either on a linotype machine or by monotype. In my judgment, a linotype machine produces a more professional appearance. The cost is often less than $14 per page, and this is most reasonable when one considers the number of copies to be printed from the initial investment in typesetting.

   After the galley proofs are returned, one set will be used to paste up a dummy. Reproductions of the illustrations are pasted in place. From this dummy, final adjustments of spacing and even rewording and resetting of the copy can be made.

4. The last step is the actual printing process. If the publication is to be printed on a letterpress, the metal is locked up in the form and printed directly onto the paper. If offset is utilized, one must obtain reproduction proofs of the type matter set. This in turn is pasted up into the exact form as it will be printed. The printer then makes a negative of the

copy and artwork; from this negative a plate is made which is utilized on the printing press to print the final work.

It is important for library friends to compete not only with the mass media, but also with the many other community interests and organizations issuing printed matter. It is imperative that publications issued by the friends evoke and stimulate the interest in the organization's activities, services, and objectives through the appeal of tasteful design. A piece of printing invariably reflects the philosophy and tone of the source producing it. Your objective is to speak in so warm, lively, and colorful a style that even the most jaded patron will see a new awareness of the importance of the library and its friends. Remember the words of Jan Tschichold:

> Perfect typography is certainly the most elusive of all arts. Out of stiff, unconnected little parts a whole must be shaped which is alive and convincing as a whole. Sculpture in stone alone comes near in its obstinacy to perfect typography. For most people it offers no special aesthetic charm as it is as difficult of access as the highest music, and in the most favourable cases is merely accepted with gratitude. The knowledge that he is rendering an anonymous service to valuable works, and to a small number of optically sensitive people, is as a rule the only reward for the typographer's long and never-ending apprenticeship.[1]

NOTE

1. Tschichold, Jan. "Clay in the Potter's Hand" (folder). In *Homage to the Book*. New York, West Virginia Pulp and Paper Co., 1968, p. 3.

JEANNE BOHLEN

Information on Foundations

There are more than 22,000 private foundations in the United States. Unfortunately, the terminology in this field is rather confusing. Many organizations which contain the name "foundation" do not meet the criteria laid down in the tax code and many of these do not make grants. There are also some foundations which do not have the word "foundation" as part of their name (e.g., Carnegie Corporation of New York, Stearns Charitable Trust). The Internal Revenue Service publishes a volume entitled *Cumulative List of Organizations Described in Section 170(c) of the Internal Revenue Code of 1954* (Internal Revenue Service Publication 78). This publication lists the organizations defined in the tax laws as private foundations. Generally speaking, a private foundation is nonprofit, nongovernmental, and governed by its own board of trustees; and it has a principal fund of its own. Such a definition unfortunately includes some organizations not included under the tax code definition. The ultimate authority is IRS Publication 78.

It is important to recognize that foundation resources are relatively small. Their assets exceed $34 billion, and each year they give away a little more than $2 billion; but compare this $2 billion to the as much as $200 billion given away by the government, or the close to $33 billion in contributions from individual persons. You can see the basic problem faced by the foundations: how to spend these relatively few dollars in a way that will have a significant impact.

Foundations are governed by the tax laws. The Tax Reform Act of 1969 was very significant for foundations; subsequent laws have made some changes. Several provisions are important to this discussion. For example, foundations now have a disclosure requirement. All are required to file tax returns that show the names of the foundation managers and a list of their grants (names of the organizations and dollar amounts). The tax returns are photographed by IRS and microfiche copies are available for purchase. People often say, "I thought all foundations were required to publish an annual report"; this process is what they have in mind. With the 1969 act came restrictions on grants to individuals. Before making such grants, foundations must create a special process to be approved by IRS. As a result, most foundations choose to make grants only to tax-exempt organizations.

Scholarship funds often go directly to a university which will, in turn, select the individual recipients. The Foundation Center has published a directory of those relatively few (about 1000) foundations that do make grants to individuals.[1] Other parts of the tax laws affect such issues as excise tax, payout requirements, gifts to organizations with IRS tax-exempt status, lobbying, investments, self-dealing, and others.

It is important to recognize the difference between the several types of foundations: independent, company-sponsored, and community. Independent foundations may be separated into general-purpose, special-purpose, and family foundations. General-purpose foundations operate under broad charters at the direction of their boards of trustees. These are usually large national foundations with enough flexibility to choose new areas of grant making. Special-purpose foundations, on the other hand, make grants within a specific area of interest, often because of the terms of the original bequest, or perhaps because of the special interest of the donor. Of the 22,000 foundations, most are family foundations; that is, they have living family members on the board helping to select the grant recipients. Family foundations come in all sizes and degrees of sophistication, from the highly staffed foundation with written guidelines and a published annual report, to the foundation whose board meets once a year and gives to the same organizations each year. Most family foundations fall between these two extremes. As you do your research it is important to note the type of foundation you will be approaching.

Corporations can meet their social responsibility in a number of ways. One is by contributing goods and services in kind; each year many millions of dollars are given in this way. Corporations can give actual dollars in a couple of ways: they can create foundations to make contributions, or they can give the money directly. When the corporation creates a foundation, the foundation must abide by the tax laws governing private foundations — disclosure, payout requirement, excise tax, etc. When it gives directly, there are no such requirements. Remember that corporations have responsibilities to their stockholders and need to justify their charitable contributions as being in the corporate interest. Often the contributions are made to communities where the corporation has employees, for public relations purposes, and to organizations supported by or serving their employees. Corporations are allowed to give up to 5 percent of their pretax profits for charitable purposes, which may be taken as a tax deduction. Overall giving by corporations in 1977 was 0.98 percent of net income before taxes.[2]

Community foundations have local giving patterns. The concept is to have monies set aside in trust and invested; the income is given back to the community in the form of grants to tax-exempt organizations. The first community foundation was the Cleveland Foundation, which is still one of the largest. Community foundations have a special tax status and are not defined as private foundations. This means they do not file the 990-AR or 990-PF tax return, do not have a payout requirement and pay no excise tax. The fact that they are not required to file the tax returns required of private foundations does not mean that they will remain hidden. In order to maintain the favorable tax status they must receive contributions each year from public sources, such as wills, individual contributions, and memorial funds. However, foundation directories that are prepared from information taken solely from the private foundation's tax returns will omit community foundations. On the other hand, many directories that focus on specific subject areas often include community foundations, even though the grants will be made in only one community. Several important points should be remembered about community foundations. If a foundation has a geographic name, suspect that it may be a community foundation. Community foundations make grants almost exclusively to organizations in their community or to organizations serving people living in their community. Usually, grants made outside the community are the result of designated funds where the donor has named the agency to receive all or part of the income. You will also need to check with the individual community foundation to find out the exact geographic limits — often a county or multi-county area.

The Foundation Center (with its main office at 888 Seventh Avenue, New York, New York 10106) is a nonprofit, public-interest organization established by private foundations in 1956 to improve the philanthropic process by providing information both to grant makers and grant seekers. It is a first place to turn for factual information on philanthropic foundations. Its resources include publications and a network of libraries. You may fill out a card to be added to the mailing list to learn of new publications. Currently, the Foundation Center publishes directories, indexes, and "how-to" books, as described in a special brochure.[3] Computer-searchable data bases are available to the public through Lockheed Information Systems and to subscribers of the Associates Program through the Foundation Center directly. The Associates Program provides telephone reference and mail-out service for a fee.

There are now more than eighty regional cooperating collections of the Foundation Center, with at least one in every state. In these collections you will find copies of all Foundation Center publications, together with copies of the tax returns (in microform) for all the private foundations in the state. Also, at least part of one staff member's time is assigned to maintain the collection and to assist users of the materials. In addition, the Foundation Center has two libraries, in New York City and Washington,

D.C., where you will find copies of the tax returns (again in microform) for all the currently active private foundations nationwide. Two field offices were opened in January 1978, in Cleveland and San Francisco, which operate libraries with the tax returns for the midwestern and western United States, respectively. A list of the regional collections and their addresses is available free of charge from the New York office. The Foundation Center receives its funding from the sale of its publications, and from grants made by foundations who believe that the more information you have, the more likely you will be to send your requests only to those foundations that might have an interest in your project.

One major problem faced by foundations is the high number of inappropriate requests (e.g., a foundation interested in medical research receiving requests from a youth center or a symphony orchestra). Estimates are that as much as 80-90 percent of all requests received by a foundation fall totally outside its area of interest.

One of the problems in requesting a grant is the lack of a single catalog listing all the foundation grants available. Instead, there is a series of publications, with each volume giving different types of information. The key word here is *pattern*. You should look at the record of past grants to determine whether the foundation's pattern of giving matches your project in terms of: (1) geography, (2) subject interest, (3) type of recipient organization, (4) type of support, and (5) dollar amount.

Try to be creative in your research. Most likely, if a foundation has funded a day-care center it probably was not for the day care itself, but rather for early childhood education, or working parents, or intercultural efforts, or perhaps even a nutrition program. You are looking for a partner; the foundation has the dollars and you have the labor and skills; *together* you can reach the same goal. In your research you should be looking for a foundation with the same goals you have. Your search strategy should involve two steps. First, identify those foundations that may have a possible interest in your project — create a rather long list. Next, study each of these foundations carefully, crossing off those that do not have a pattern of giving that matches your project. The basic Foundation Center publications available for this search process are listed below. As you look through them, read the introductions carefully to see what is and is not included.

1. *The Foundation Directory* (7th edition): Gives basic descriptions of foundations with assets of $1 million or more and/or total annual grants of $100,000 or more. Only about 15 percent of the foundations are included, but these foundations own 93 percent of the assets and give 92 percent of the grant dollars.

2. *The Foundation Grants Index 1978:* Lists grants of $5000 or more made by nearly 400 foundations.
3. *COMSEARCH Printouts:* Computer searches of grants in *The Foundation Grants Index* by fifty-nine subjects.
4. *Foundation News:* A bimonthly magazine published by the Council on Foundations and the Foundation Center. The Foundation Center section contains the current listings of grants, which are cumulated into the annual volume of *The Foundation Grants Index.*
5. *Source Book Profiles:* A bimonthly looseleaf subscription service which gives detailed analyses of the 1000 largest foundations, as measured by annual grant amounts.
6. *National Data Book:* Lists the 22,000 active private foundations, gives name, address, principal officer, and fiscal information, but no subject information.

Other documents you may wish to examine include:

1. Annual reports: These are published by less than 500 of the 22,000 active private foundations; the format varies. In addition to being held by various libraries, copies are usually sent free of charge upon request to the foundation.
2. State foundation directories: Prepared by many different types of publishers, these contain much variety in format and date of information and are available for about forty states.
3. Tax returns: These are available for all currently active private foundations; they give name, address, principal officer, foundation managers, list of grants awarded, grants approved for future payment, etc.

In summary, there are many foundations in the United States. Their funds are limited, but they can have a significant impact on a library program. You must believe in your project and search for appropriate foundations with goals similar to yours.

NOTES

1. Kurzig, Carol, ed. *Foundation Grants to Individuals.* 2d ed. New York, Foundation Center, 1979.

2. Troy, Kathryn. *Annual Survey of Corporate Contributions, 1977.* New York, Conference Board, Division of Public Affairs Research, 1979.

3. "The Foundation Center." New York, Foundation Center, March 1978. (brochure)

CONTRIBUTORS

SCOTT BENNETT is Associate Professor of Library Administration and Special Collections Consultant for the University of Illinois Library. He is active in the American Association of University Professors, and is a charter member of the University of Illinois Library Friends, as well as its Secretary/Treasurer since 1972. A specialist in the history of books and periodicals, of libraries, and of reading in nineteenth-century Great Britain, he received a 1978-79 Fellowship of the American Council of Learned Societies for research on the English publisher, Charles Knight.

JEANNE BOHLEN is a field office representative of the Foundation Center, in charge of the Foundation Center-Cleveland offices. From 1972 to 1977 she was in the Reference Department of the Kansas City (Missouri) Public Library, where her work as supervisor of the Missouri-Kansas Foundation Center Regional Collection included participation in a special program on grants with the Junior League of Kansas City. Her current activities include work with the Women and Foundations/Corporate Philanthropy and the presentation of foundation grants seminars being offered by the Foundation Center under a grant received by the McDonald's Corporation.

MARIANNE G. BRISCOE is Director of Development at the Newberry Library, Chicago. Her research has specialized in medieval English rhetoric and drama; she is the recipient of a doctorate from the Catholic University of America and a British Academy Fellowship. She has been active in the work of groups ranging from the Citizens for a New Charter in Flint, Michigan, and the United Way of Chicago, to the Medieval Academy of America and the National Society of Fund Raising Executives.

SANDY DOLNICK is President of Friends of Libraries U.S.A., and editor of the *Friends of the Library National Notebook* and the *Friends of the Library Sourcebook*. From 1973 to 1979 she was editor of the newsletter of the Bookfellows of the Milwaukee Public Library, and from 1975 to 1979 she was co-president of that friends group. She has also been associated with the Public Television Auction Cabinet. She is currently a member of the board of the Friends of Wisconsin Libraries (FOWL).

EDWARD G. HOLLEY is Dean of the School of Library Science at the University of North Carolina at Chapel Hill. A distinguished library historian and author of a prize-winning biography of Charles Evans, he was President of the American Library Association during the centenary year of 1976. During his incumbency as Director of Libraries at the University of Houston, the friends group there was founded, and its journal, *Aldus,* was begun.

WILLIAM R. HOLMAN is former Director of the Rosenberg Library, Galveston, Texas (1954-56), of the San Antonio Public Library (1956-60), and of the San Francisco Public Library (1960-67). Since 1967 he has been at the University of Texas at Austin, originally with the Humanities Research Center, and more recently in the Graduate School of Library Science. Formerly a Councilor of the American Library Association, he was also President of the Friends of Libraries Committee. His notable career as a book designer is reflected in his book, *Library Publications* (1965).

TEM HORWITZ is Director of Lawyers for the Creative Arts in Chicago, and is active in the development and management of philanthropic activities in the arts. His writings include four books: *Sweet Home Chicago* (1976), *Tai Chi Ch'uan* (1977), *Arts Administration* (1978), and *Law & the Arts: Art & the Law* (1980).

D.W. KRUMMEL is Professor of Library Science at the University of Illinois, specializing in general, music, and historical bibliography. Author of six books and numerous articles, he was a Guggenheim Fellow in 1976-77. He is President-Elect of the Music Library Association, and an adjunct member of the School of Music faculty at Illinois. In the 1960s he was Associate Librarian of the Newberry Library, during the time of the founding of the Newberry Library Associates; and at Illinois he was a founder of the University of Illinois Library Friends, as well as the first president of its Executive Committee.

ANNE J. MATHEWS is a member of the Friends of Libraries U.S.A. Executive Board, and Associate Professor and Director of Continuing Education at the Graduate School of Librarianship and Information Management of the University of Denver. Her doctoral work was in the field of interpersonal communication, and her writings have specialized in management studies and systems analysis. A past president of the Colorado Library Association, she is now an ALA Councilor and Secretary of the Board of Continuing Library Education Network and Exchange (CLENE), as well as a member of the Board of Managers of the Friends of the Denver Public Library.

PAUL H. MOSHER is Associate Director for Collection Development of the Stanford University Libraries. His background as a scholar has been in the field of medieval European history; more recently, he has written in the field of collection development and management. Formerly Chairman of the Chief Collection Development Officers of Large Research Libraries Discussion Group, he is now Chair-Elect of the Resources Section of the Resources and Technical Services Division of ALA.

THOMAS G. SANBERG is Vice President for Marketing and Plant Development of Henrotin Hospital, Chicago. He is also Vice President of the Chicago Chapter of the National Association of Fund Raising Executives, as well as an officer of the group's national Board of Directors. His former development activities include work with the Allendale School for Boys, the Chicago Educational Television Association (WTTW, Channel 11), and the Community Television Foundation of South Florida (WPBT, Channel 2), and duties as vice president of the firm of Charles R. Feldstein, Inc.

ELAINE SEATON is Director of the Manhasset Public Library, Manhasset, New York. Previously she was the first Director of the library at the newly founded State University of New York College at Old Westbury. Active in numerous professional organizations, she is on the Executive Board of Friends of Libraries U.S.A. and is Vice President of the Chamber of Commerce in Manhasset.

CYNTHIA WEDEL has been active in the work of the Protestant Episcopal Church, and more recently, of the National Council of Churches; since 1975 she has served as a President of the World Council of Churches. Her distinguished career has included membership on the National Board of the Girl Scouts of America (1960-66) and the President's Commission for the Status of Women (1961-63); work as Associate Director of the Center for a Volunteer Society (1969-74) and on the Executive Board of the National Urban Coalition; and, since 1969, work as a consultant on volunteers for the American Red Cross. Her writings include *Employed Women and the Church* (1969) and *Faith and Fear and Future Shock* (1974).

INDEX

Administration, of development activity, 79

Ambrosiana Library (Milan), 23

Area bibliographers. *See* Subject bibliographers

Arts, The, and library friends, 35

Ashendene Press, 104-05

Audit, organizational, 78-79

Babb, James T., 9

Baskerville, John, 104

Beinecke family, 9

Benefits to donors, 97-102

Benton, Charles, 48

Bodley, Sir Thomas, 27

Book and author programs, 34

Book sales, 34

Borromeo, Cardinal Federigo, 23

Brochures, 82

Budgeting, as part of development, 79

Carnegie, Andrew, 25

Communications with public. *See* Public relations

Community foundations. *See* Foundations, community

Community liaison, 82

Corporations, as donors, 110-11

Council for Florida Libraries, 46

Davis, Maude, 23

Design of publications, aesthetics of, 103-05

Deus ex machina fallacy of friends board recruitment, 87

Development: administration of, 79; relation of, to organizational structure, 77-78

Development work in libraries, 74-75

Doms, Keith, 52

Donor acquisition, 80

Donor renewal, 80

Doren, Mark Van, 27

Doves Press, 104

Dudley, Fredrica Gross, 21

Duggan, Maryann, 49

Evans, Emily Scott, 12-13

Ewarts' 1850 library bill, 24-25

Family foundations. *See* Foundations, independent

Financial support, myths of, 19-20

Foundation Center, 111-12

Foundations: community, 110-11; family, *see* Foundations, independent; general purpose, *see* Foundations, independent; independent, 110; private, definition of, 109; resources of, 109; tax laws applied to, 109-10; types of, 110

FOWL. *See* Friends of Wisconsin Libraries, Inc.

Friends: benefits derived from history of, 30-31; reasons for lack of history of, 26-28; sustaining interest of, 97-102

Friends governing board. *See* Governing board of friends

Friends groups: activities of, in academic libraries, 70; administration of, 87; and subject bibliographers, 73-74; case studies of, 58-66; characteristics of, 57-58, 69; evaluation of, 85-86; goals and objectives of, 42-43, 70; identification of members for, 98-99; at national level, *see* Friends of Libraries U.S.A.; organization and governance of, 43; profile of, 33-34; role of, 72-73; at state level, 43-46

Friends of California Libraries, 45

Friends of Libraries U.S.A., 33, 38, 47, 51

Friends of the Denver Public Library, 41

Friends of the Library of Columbia University, 27